The Blue Bottles Writing Studio

An Anthology

Written and Edited by Members of the
Blue Bottles Writing Studio

Sita C. Amba-Rao
George Francis Edward
Elizabeth Jane Pryce
Sandra J. S. Stanton

Village Books Publishing
Bellingham, Washington, 2020

ISBN: 978-0-578-65829-2

Library of Congress Control Number: 2020905066

Book Design by Jill Flores
Cover Artwork by David W. Wakeling

Printed by Village Books Publishing

First printing edition 2020

Village Books
1200 11th Street
Bellingham, WA 98225

Introduction

$\mathcal{T}$he Blue Bottles Writing Studio was started by Elizabeth Jane Pryce in the summer of 2018 as an activity of Bellingham at Home, a volunteer organization that provides transportation and other help for members who need it, as well as social and creative activities.

We are a small group of four independent writers who come together once a week to share our creativity; Sita C. Ambro-Rao, George Francis Edward, Elizabeth Jane Pryce and Sandra J. S. Stanton. Our writing has evolved over time. We've gathered together our favorites in this anthology: Creative Memoirs, Stories from a Photograph, Short Stories, Scribblings, and The Newspaper Challenge.

Creative Memoirs are stories where each member was free to choose a topic of significance in their personal life. We shared these stories in the second half of our weekly sessions.

Stories from a Photograph was the most recent addition to our writing. Each member in turn presented a photograph, without comment or description, from which we created our own stories to fit the photograph. The last piece following each photograph tells the true story.

Short Stories are writing pieces prompted by a single word or phrase. Each member had a turn selecting the word prompt to be used as writing inspiration at the next meeting.

Scribblings are short pieces, written within a five–seven minute timeframe, based around five words generated by an internet random word generator. Each word must be included to create a fun little story.

The Newspaper Challenge was started by an idea that Elizabeth Jane Pryce came up with, the odd storyline phase like, "Its Like Wearing Clown Shoes or Something", because she was curious to see what each member would write. Happily, the challenge was taken on by the all of the members.

Acknowledgments

$\mathcal{F}$irstly, the Blue Bottles Writing Studio, both collectively and individually, would like to thank the members for their weekly enthusiasm and support, without which, this book could not have come to fruition.

We would like to thank Joan Dow for participating in our writing sessions—although she elected not to publish.

We also thank Jill Flores, our graphic designer, for her patience and professional approach.

Thank you to Dana Lyon Edward for the individual member photographs and group photograph on the back cover.

A big thank you to Sandra J. S. Stanton for all her hard work editing.

I personally would like to thank my son, David Wakeling, for providing the original cover artwork and my granddaughter, Millyn Moose Moss, and a few other close friends for proofreading my stories.

Elizabeth Jane Pryce
Founder of The Blue Bottles Writing Studio
Spring 2020

Contents

Creative Memoirs

Memoirs taken from our writers' widely varied lives.

FAMILY HISTORY: MY FATHER

Sita C. Amba-Rao

*M*y father's family comes from a village in a state in India where rice fields are in abundance. The water source comes from the mighty Godavari River. The family is of Brahmin caste, which is at the top of the hierarchic caste system in India. Traditionally, this caste is of the priest class, with emphasis on formal learning. Wealth is not a characteristic; in fact, the Brahmins are of very modest means, rich in respect but poor in wealth. The family possessed some agricultural property, but it was not of much significance.

In the early 20th century, going to school for my dad required walking some distance, then taking a ferry across the river, then walking some more. There was no electricity in small towns, he had to study by a hurricane lantern. My dad was persistent in his studies. After high school he went on to college in a nearby city. Then he proceeded to graduate school in a more distant university, for which his family had to sell part of their land. Afterwards he returned to his home state and began teaching in the college where he originally received his Bachelor's degree. His ambitions did not stop there; he received a grant to study abroad in England. Noticing his potential and passion, his family sold more of their land, and sent him on his pursuit with their blessings. He successfully completed his study, earning a PhD degree in Chemical Technology at Liverpool University, a reputable school in that era. He then returned to India.

During his studies in England, Dad left behind a wife and two young children; my older brother, Ravi and me. My mother and dad were cousins. My mom lived with her children near one of my dad's brothers, while my dad was away. All of us cousins had a great time, with little of it spent in school at that age. Mostly, I remember monkeying around! Literally, dodging and running for safety from monkeys trying to snatch our food. The city of Tirupathi, was well known for the great hilltop temple of Lord Venkateswara, the deity of many families; a busy place of pilgrimage. It must have been the constant availability of bananas offered to the God, which drew the monkey population to that place. People would leave them alone to wander as they pleased, as long as they did not enter their homes.

When Dad came home, he was subjected to a purification process, one of the social rituals of that time, for folks returning from living abroad. It was very ceremonial, almost like a wedding, welcoming the returning son as the proverbial "prodigal son." Accepting him back into the community, and reuniting him with his wife and family. This evoked such excitement in me that I went around announcing that my dad and mom were getting married! My brother and I were around six and four years of age, respectively at that time!

Soon thereafter, my family began a series of moves to the large urban cities of Calcutta, Bombay and, finally, to Hyderabad. Dad found well-paying jobs in private industry, which provided a comfortable life style for us, during those years. We were a happy family. My dad, young and full of energy, worked happily and hard in his occupation. My mom stayed home taking care of her two children as they were growing up. My parents were quite fashionably and elegantly dressed for those days. I fondly remember how my mom curled my bobbed hair with a hot iron rod folded in a piece of cloth. This idyllic situation did not last for long, however. A year after we moved to Hyderabad, my mom contracted the deadly disease of those days; asthma, for which there was no cure. She was only 29 years old. My younger brother, Mohan was born in Hyderabad. He was barely a year old when my mom died. Ironically, this was the same city to which my dad moved his family after another epochal period abroad, in the United States of America. He would spend the last few years of his life in Hyderabad, where he passed away in the 1960s.

My mother knew she was dying. She was in the hospital. My dad carried the burden alone for some time, until an aunt, his oldest brother's widow, and her daughter, in her late teens, came to live with and take care of us. In anticipation of my aunt's arrival, my mother tried to prepare us to be in our aunt's care. On one occasion, when we visited our mum in the hospital, she asked me to sit closer to her. I was so afraid of the hospital, with people lying ill in their beds, that I was afraid to go near my mother. With her feeble, but endearing voice, she told me that my auntie would be taking care of us. She told me that we would be happy. We would go to school and study hard. Those were the last words I heard from my mother. Gripped with fear, I showed no emotion. Soon after, she passed away.

Thinking back, with sadness, I wonder how many young women died in the prime of their youth, for lack of medical treatment, before having the pleasure of seeing their children grow up and cherishing them.

When a wife dies before her husband, there are customs and rituals to be followed, on a scale depending on the wealth and belief of the individuals. While my dad did follow certain practices out of tradition and respect for my mother and her family, I believe, he kept it simple. In contrast, I should mention what used to happen when a husband died, leaving his wife. Many around the world would have heard about the infamous sacrificial pyre to which the young wife was subjected. That practice, known as Sati, was finally outlawed in the late 19th century.

If the wife died first she was treated with ceremony. Her body bathed, smeared with turmeric, and draped in new clothes. She was adorned with *tilak** and appropriate jewelry—all of them, indicating the wife's journey, as she leaves her body to await her husband, who will join her after death.

Some family members came from out of town for the occasion, but I do not remember seeing my mother's parents. The reason may have been, either my grandfather was ill and my grandmother had to take care of him, or perhaps, for another, totally different reason. There is a belief among Indians, Hindus in particular, that any significant event should be undertaken at an auspicious time—that is, following certain astronomical contexts, good and bad omens. Accordingly, my mother was to return home to her family after her last child was born. My grandmother came up with an auspicious date. My dad, being a non-believer, insisted on an earlier date. Adamantly he brought my mother home much against my grandmother's wishes. My grandmother even predicted that, if my mother left her home on that date, she would never see her again alive. As it happened, unfortunately, that came true. Perhaps for that reason, my grandmother did not set foot in our house again, until many years later.

Still in his mid-thirties, my Dad was left a widower, with three young children to raise. My aunt and cousin helped him for another three years, until he married my second mother, Lakshmi.

* *Tilak* is traditionally the red dot on the forehead of a Hindu married woman.

WONDER OF WATER

Sita C. Amba-Rao

*T*he serene flow of water is solace to the soul and calming to the mind.

For twenty years my husband, Chintskindi Lalitha, known as CL, and I planned to move to San Diego on my retirement, in the year 2000. Preferably, near the shore, to the north of the city. We imagined a peaceful life with a view of the water, dotted by frequent surfers and other beach goers of all ages. The year before my retirement, however, CL's visit with his sister Rama and brother-in-law, TK, in Vancouver, BC changed that idyllic plan. They drove him to Bellingham in Washington, 55 miles south of Vancouver and a hundred miles north of Seattle. They showed him around, and they sent me an article on Bellingham, from the local newspaper. CL was impressed and came back with a desire to choose Bellingham over San Diego. On reading the article, I too was drawn to the exotic, hidden gem, nestled between the two major metro areas of Seattle and Vancouver.

The city was close to the Canadian border, with a free flow of visitors between the two sister cities. More than anything, what jumped out at me, on reading the article, was a small incident. A retiree weekly travelled the twenty miles south between Blaine on the US and Canada border and Fairhaven, a village within Bellingham, to a local bookstore, got a book, went to the café next door and enjoyed the afternoon with her book and coffee.

I later found out that both the bookstore and the cafe were iconic figures in Fairhaven, and were busy with customers all day. Good co-branding for the stores and a smart marketing move. So, that was it—my "aha!" moment for the switch from San Diego to Bellingham.

It was about two years later, however that I had an occasion to consider what it really was about this quiet little town that anchored us. A national financial magazine's reporter was in town interviewing a few "old" and "new" residents, inquiring what it was about living in Bellingham, that attracted us. Amongst the interviewees, were my neighbor and us. My neighbor described her highlight as, having neighbors of a different culture who, when they celebrated their 50th wedding anniversary, invited her to the occasion. This had thrilled her and given her a learning experience. Those neighbors were us, with a gathering of 25 family members and friends.

As newcomers from the Midwest flatlands, to the exquisite beauty of the Pacific northwest, our take was different. We were blown away by the evergreen territorial landscape in the foreground and the view of the Bellingham Bay, from our condo, with mountains all around. The night view reminded us of Manhattan, at least, in our imagination. Our wedding anniversary was a "picnic in the park" at at Bloedel Donovan Park on Lake Whatcom, on a sunny afternoon. There were wonderful shadows dancing among the trees. The crescent shaped lake was full of boaters, and children dipping into the shallow waters at one end. The backdrop to all of this, was a mountainous terrain covered with evergreen pines and firs.

With this perspective in mind, my rhetorical question to the reporter was, "Where else can you find a small town where an ocean and a lake co-exist, a valley couched among hills and a view of snow covered mountains as a backdrop; especially Mt. Baker." This was our home! These natural wonders, along with the holy Ganges in India, embrace the remains of my life partner, CL. They offer him the means to become one with the Universe.

LA PAVILION
Western's Newest Sculpture

George Francis Edward

If you have never worked for a university, you will have no idea what I am talking about. The university was created in medieval times and developed during the middle ages. If the university did not already exist, you could not create one today.

I worked for Western Washington University for almost seven years. I paid my dues. I know how a university works. The crux of the university system is power. Tenured faculty have power. Department chairs have power. Deans have power. Everybody else is powerless, including the students.

La Pavilion

When the faculty interact with the lowly staff employees, it's like a mighty lawnmower versus a lowly garden slug. Why? Because slugs have no power. They can be squished, poisoned, or in the case of the garden slugs in my yard, minced into a disgusting brown jelly.

Tenured faculty enjoy the privileges of the university system as long as they live. It must be nice to know that no matter how badly you screw up on your job, you will always have it in the morning. But, like I said, the university system was created for the powerful. Not for garden slugs or worthless schlumps in accounting like me.

I worked in the Business Services Department at Western Washington University. This meant my department received the invoices, paid the bills, and issued payroll checks. Pretty boring stuff. But still important, or so we thought. We thought our jobs had meaning, but we were just fooling ourselves. The President of Western Washington University decided to relocate "nonessential employees" off campus. All employees in the Business Services Department were deemed "nonessential." If you weren't a tenured professor, department chair, or a dean, the President declared you were "nonessential" and you should be moved off the Western campus.

Our department was moved off campus to 32nd Street Bellingham, WA, and housed in a small brick building. My office was the window on the left in the photograph. At 32nd Street, we were treated to constant homeless encounters. It got so bad we found the homeless using our bathroom and taking a shower. We created a security card system so that only the staff employees could enter the doors. We used the buddy system at night for escorts to our cars.

Our 32nd Street employee 'break room' had no refrigerator, no microwave, no chairs, no tables, no knives or forks, frankly, nothing. We were told, if we wanted these things, the staff should buy them with their own money. The university was not going to spend taxpayer funds on "nonessential employees."

I think my biggest problem was looking out the window of my office and seeing the trash left by the homeless. If I were on the university campus, this wouldn't be tolerated. The campus security would not allow the homeless to set up shop in the middle of the university. But this rule did not apply to our office, since we were "off campus" and we had no security service patrolling our parking lot.

I stared out my window at the abandoned shopping cart in the photo for months. I kept waiting for somebody to move it away from our parking lot, but it never happened. The shopping cart was here to stay. It had tenure. Then it occurred to me. The abandoned shopping cart was part of Western's acclaimed Sculpture Garden! Why didn't I think of this sooner!?!

Rather than look away from the hideous shopping cart, I embraced it as a critically acclaimed steel sculpture. Although untitled, and by an unknown artist, the sculpture had the word "Pavilion" engraved on the red plastic handle. Even though Pavilion was the name of a local supermarket, I assumed the anonymous artist was referring to a "Pavilion" which is the bottom portion of a cut gemstone, beginning at the girdle and going to the point at its lower end. Indeed, "La Pavilion" was our gem!

For purposes of art appraisal, we showed a photo of the shopping cart sculpture to local art critics. They agreed that *La Pavilion* "*gives an illusion of space and time and, yet, tenderly embraces the notion of quality food at affordable prices.*"

One art critic stated, "*A perceptual experience, La Pavilion is a rejection of rationality and, unlike other sculptures on the Western campus, it allows the viewer to contemplate the union of physical action, intellectual thinking and fresh produce.*" The critic concluded: "**La Pavilion** *sets up an important metaphysical dialogue between the checkout line and the trunk of your car.*"

Another critic observed "*The unknown artist skillfully fashions* **La Pavilion** *in hand wrought steel, highly polished, which intrinsically mimics Titian's Three Ages of Man.*" The critic continued "*La Pavilion expresses the relationship between our inner and outer selves. It is a metaphoric bridge between what in life is true, the forms of nature and a spill on aisle twelve.*"

The Western community was invited to comment on our newest and most mysterious sculpture. But nobody ever came to view our glittering outdoor art installation. One day the shopping cart just disappeared. I was told that a homeless person was using it to store all of his worldly possessions.

What a philistine!! What a barbarian!!

It was obvious this person never studied Art at a prestigious university like Western.

THE PRANKSTER

George Francis Edward

$\mathcal{I}$n his hand, our neighbor Grant is holding a red tail-light from a bicycle. He sneaked over to our house, and duck taped this light onto our kitchen window then set the flasher so it would pulsate constantly. The problem with his little trick was that it was the Summer Solstice, the longest day of the year. When there is full sunlight, you can't see the faint flashing light. Since Grant taped it to the corner of our kitchen window, I never noticed it, because I failed to enter our kitchen in the evening—when it was dark outside. Not only that, I am told by my wife that I am not very observant! So the blinking light was taped to our house for almost a full week!

Finally, Dana noticed the flashing light when she was in the kitchen. It scared her until she realized who placed it there! I walked over to Grant and handed the tail-light to him. "Please hold this flashing light so I can take a photo. I'll need it as evidence when I go to court and file a restraining order against you!"

I have known Grant over twenty years. He is a "wise guy." Grant's mother called him a "wise ass," this epithet fits him to a tee. Grant goes through life looking for ways to prank people. Unfortunately, since I am Grant's neighbor, I am the brunt of more than my share of his practical jokes.

After Grant replaced the toilet in his rental house, he drove home and put the old toilet bowl on display in the middle of my lawn. He told me it was a "porcelain sculpture."

Grant loves to place signs on my lawn. One day I came home and found a "Grant for Mayor" sign. Another time he placed a "Save the Orcas" sign on my lawn. I can be fairly sure that if Grant comes across a random sign, he is going to steal it and stick it on my front lawn. The sign's message is immaterial.

Grant often rides his motorcycle onto my lawn, then rides in a circle doing "donuts."

However, I am partially to blame. I now realize that Grant has the maturity of a five-year-old boy. If I give him a toy, he will play with it. Case in point: my old mailbox. Grant helped me install a new mailbox and I foolishly handed him the old mailbox. This was a serious mistake on my part, I soon realized. I came home and found my old mailbox nailed to a tree about twenty feet in the air. Grant painted on the side of the mailbox "Air Mail."

I walked over to Grant's house and told him to get that stupid mailbox off my tree! Again, I am totally to blame. Why would I give an uncontrollable juvenile delinquent an old mailbox? My bad.

Grant loves to decorate my car with various signs and slogans. I woke up one morning and noticed a large 'TAXI' sign on the top of my car. On another occasion, Grant placed a large 'STUDENT DRIVER' sign on the car.

Grant regularly doctors my license plate. Once he changed the "University of Pennsylvania" license plate to read "University of Penis-lyvania." Thankfully, he used masking tape so I could easily remove the offending language.

I have to be careful of letting my car windows get dirty. Grant sneaks over to my yard and writes messages on the back window of my car. One time he wrote, "Black Lives Matter" in the dust. I drove the car for several days with this message before I noticed it. I have accepted the fact that Grant writes messages on my vehicle whatever he feels like it. It's kind of an open canvas for his bizarre personality.

Because Grant is obsessed with playing pranks on me, he notices everything I do. If I park my car in a different spot on the driveway, he places a yellow sign on the window. Grant loves beer, so the penalty is usually fairly minor, like one Bud Lite beer.

Ticket! Parking on driveway not in designated spot! Penalty / Beer

I made the mistake of installing a game camera in my yard. I was curious to see the kinds of nocturnal animals browsing on my property. Guess which animal showed up first? You guessed it. I wonder if the gentle forest animals can detect strange human behavior?

Of course, Grant's pranks are all in good fun. He is fortunate I have a good sense of humor. However, Grant cannot control his pranks, because there is basically a screw loose in his head. I say this with all seriousness. The man needs a therapist! He needs months on a couch with extensive psychological study and treatment! Grant needs a brain rewiring; or at the very minimum, a frontal lobotomy. One particular recurrent abnormal behavior is worth mentioning: Grant loves to sneak onto my property while I am leaf blowing, or weed whacking, and pull the extension cord from the electrical socket. He gets a big thrill out of watching me take off my headphones, and safety glasses, and walk over to the electrical box to reattach the extension cord.

Grant has been pulling my electric cord (figuratively and literally) for **over twenty years**. He *still* finds it amusing. I now leaf blow or weed whack only on Wednesdays, because on that beautiful day, Grant is busy helping his wife, Mary, mind their grandchildren.

IS IT WEDNESDAY YET?

As a result, I love Wednesdays. I made a red button, which I showed to Grant. I told him I look forward to Wednesdays because, on that day, I am totally free from the giant pain in the ass (namely, my neighbor). Grant agrees with me. He said he wouldn't want himself for a neighbor, either!

AN OLD GREEN BICYCLE

Elizabeth Jane Pryce

When Daddy came home one day with my first grown-up bicycle hanging unceremoniously out of the Citroen, I was very happy. I wanted to get on it immediately and pedal away into the sunset! I was a young romantic dreamer in those days!

"Oh no, just wait a minute my girl. First I will overhaul it and clean it and make sure everything is working and you are going to help me. Then you can do it the next time."

We cleared the living room floor, which fortunately was concrete! "Make sure you roll that carpet up, Clem, and don't spill any oil on the floor!" Mummy said, as she handed us an old worn bed sheet to lay down first. "And you pay attention to your father, Janie, he'll do a good job."

Daddy handed me some special bike spanners and showed me how to fit them over the nuts and start undoing them. He also gave me the best advice I have ever had. We laid out all the nuts, bolts and other pieces of the bike as we undid them, in a direct line from where we had taken them off the bicycle. We created a template on the floor for putting every part of the bicycle back together correctly.

Daddy spent the better part of two or three days going over everything with me. He didn't go out into the fields or go down the road and come home drunk. Mummy made bread as usual and gave us big warm slices slathered with home-churned butter. Delicious! I remember that once or twice we danced a jig of *hands, knees and boomp-a daisy*, around the living room and out into the kitchen, where Daddy gave Mummy a kiss on the back of the neck and twirled her around. She would always shake him off with a laugh.

Learning to ride the bicycle was a big hurdle for me. I could steer well, but I just couldn't seem to balance, mainly because I was afraid of falling off onto the stony road where we lived! It took Daddy, when he could, and various friends, several days running alongside me, before I finally mastered the art!

Have you ever had the feeling that someone was beside you, but actually they weren't? That's how it happened! I was so engrossed in keeping my head up, looking ahead, holding the handlebars straight, pedaling constantly, to stay on the bicycle, to realize that Noel, my good friend Gloria's brother, was no longer holding my saddle and running beside me. He had let go of the bike some 50 yards further back. When I discovered he wasn't there, I promptly, and in an ungraceful fashion, fell off!

"Why did you let go," I shouted back at him.

"You were ready," was all he said, when he got to my side and helped me up. "Now, get back on and ride."

Noel steadied the bicycle while I put my foot through the frame, hoisted myself up onto the saddle and said, "OK, push me off." I was off and away this time, wobbling a little at first, but I did not fall!

Suddenly my world opened up. I could be gone all day and still get home in time for dinner. After a bit more practice, I might be allowed to ride to school. I would no longer be embarrassed by the bus driver refusing to let me onto the bus, because Daddy hadn't paid him. Or having to stand in the road and hail down some passing car to take me to school. I could go to the Aquatic Club now without waiting for Daddy to take me and I could visit friends in town. I was so excited!

By the end of the summer I had persuaded Mummy to let me ride to school. I learned to put my skirt over the saddle so that the pleats wouldn't be crinkled, by the time I reached school. The nuns would discipline us if we arrived at school with our clothes in a crumpled state!

It was a long ride, five miles to be exact. Down the river bed road from my house to the post office at the main road. Turn right and keep on going up the hill to the Aquatic Club, and then on to Indian Bay. I always looked for the big white cross, where old man, DeFreitas is buried.* The idea of being buried upright in a large

---

* Sylvester Gonslaves DeFreitas was buried on Dove Island in a standing position within a huge white cross. He was a man of exceptional vision and outstanding businessman. He was one of St. Vincent's first entrepreneurs. His main concern was transforming the way of life in St. Vincent. His pleasures were women; fathering as many as 52 children, the first 10 with his wife. His vices smoking; an average of 200 a day!

He made elaborate plans for his death, securing a 99 year lease of Dove Island off the coast of Indian Bay. He had his coffin built, years before he passed, trying it out for comfort, before he was satisfied

www.youtube.com/watch?v=XKw4aESuPMc

hollow cross, filled me with awe! From there, it was downhill to the airstrip, then a mere dirt track. There were no barriers, and I had to watch for the planes taxiing over the road ready for takeoff. I often wondered what would happen if I were half way across and a plane started to take off!

After that, it was a long slow climb up Arnos Vale Hill, past the cigarette factory and on up past the old house where Aunty Gussie lived and the glorious moment when I reached the top. I always stood a while and looked down over the bay. I could see the ships in the harbor off to the left below me, and Kingstown to the right. I would be at school in just a few minutes.

Thank goodness Mummy had no reservations about letting me ride a bicycle in public, wearing trousers, or shorts if I was going to the beach. There were a few people who complained to her that it wasn't ladylike for me to ride a bicycle; they were afraid it would develop muscles in the wrong places!

This old green bicycle, which I had originally seen in my Aunty Gussie's dusty old cellar while I was playing at her house, became my best friend for the next few years until I left the island. It allowed me the freedom to go places independently, which was a powerful experience.

MOUNTAIN WATER

Elizabeth Jane Pryce

*T*he man who came to the house that morning had black leathery skin. He wore an old blue shirt with cut off sleeves and khaki pants tied at the waist with coarse rope, his name was Thomas. His dog, Billie, was a black and white border collie mongrel mix. He had alert eyes, a mouth always open in a wide grin and a very happily wagging tail! When I saw them coming up the steps to the front door, I ran outside immediately to play with Billie. I really wanted a dog of my own.

Thomas called though the house to Mummy, "Mornin' Missus, canna take ya childe up moun'ain with me this mornin'? It be lovely toda!"

Thomas had a small red and white checkered bundle tied to a stick, which he carried over his shoulder. "I'zz got the vittles, Missus."

Mummy always said yes and I was already wearing brown shorts, a blue flowered blouse with a Peter Pan collar, I only had to shove my feet into my old leather-soled Clark's sandals.

We were off on an exciting adventure by eight-thirty on a summer morning. I walked next to Thomas, not talking much, in the already bright sunshine. Billie trotted quietly at Thomas' side.

At the end of our land was an old stone cottage, where Ryan, when he wasn't too drunk, sometimes worked for Daddy. He lived with his woman and son, little Willie. The air around their house was filled with the pungent smell of pigs rooting in the dirt outback. Willie's woman was squatting out front by an open fire, feeding and singing a bawdy song to the baby.

A little further up the road lived my best friends, Gloria and Noel and their two little sisters. They kept chickens, ducks and goats for food and milk. I liked going there to play, because it was so different from my home. At Christmas time, their mother would make Christmas Cake and Pudding in a galvanized bath tub! I remember how it took both the two smallest children together to turn the spoon in the mixture.

Thomas, Billie and I walked on for what seemed about an hour or more, before we stopped outside a rundown, shanty building with a long wooden bench on the outside, where a few very old men were sitting smoking their pipes. Through the door I could see a long counter, behind which were shelves stacked with canned goods.

I had been this far from home once before, and a woman had brought me some bread and cheese to eat. Her throaty laugh and demand that I stay outside had made me nervous at first, but the bread and cheese was so different from anything I had ever had at home, and very good. It was island food; it smelled like the warm sweet air itself, had a salty taste like the sea and seemed full of unknown mystery!

Now, with Thomas, I went inside. It was dark and musty. An old rusty Frigidaire hummed in the corner. Inside it, was ice cream, the salty yellow butter and the bright orange tangy cheese made by the women of the hills.

The woman's loud throaty laugh broke the silence. "Where ye be goin' wid dem white gal To'mas? She be too young for the likes of ye."

"Hush ye mouth woman, and gimme two bread and cheese for the journey."

I stayed close to Thomas and watched while she took two bread rolls from under the counter, sliced them in half with a large knife and smothered them with the yellow butter and a chunk of cheese before wrapping them up in brown paper.

"Tank ye Sadie, I'll be seeing ye later," Thomas said.

Sadie laughed in her deep voice, "Sure ye will, me man, sure ye will."

"Come child, let be goin' let git back into the clean air." Thomas said.

The rocky, dusty road was no longer accessible to vehicles, and I wondered if the native people used donkeys up in the mountains. The few people I saw in this part of the island seemed different, older, craggier and wore different clothes.

After leaving the shanty shop the trees grew more and more dense, forming a heavy canopy overhead making it dark and mysterious all around us as we walked. It was nice to feel Billie walking next to me in this part of the forest.

Eventually we left the rocky ravine and moved out into the warm sunshine. We climbed slowly across and up a grassy slope. Trees were sparse now, but huge and spreading. My favorite was the tamarind tree, with its lacy leaves and brown sweet-sour fruit hanging down from the branches like many-waisted worms. There were a few large, grass-hugging boulders scattered across the meadow.

We stopped by an outcropping. Thomas unfolded the red and white checkered cloth and took out two small glasses and a large bone, which he threw to Billie. He placed the bread and cheese on the cloth and told me to follow him. On the other side of the boulder was a tiny trickle of water, which Thomas let fall into the glass, "Now drink," he said handing me the glass.

"It's fizzy!" I exclaimed.

"Real mountain water," Thomas replied. "Us'll eat now."

We sat on the grass together, a white child and an old black man and his dog, eating and looking way off into the distant valley below, at peace with ourselves and the world.

THE HUMMINGBIRD FAMILY

Sandra J. S. Stanton

*I*n the spring of 1986, we were living in a developed community of San Diego called Tierra Santa, set on the high end of a mesa, about ten miles inland. The name means Holy Land in Spanish, undoubtedly with reference to the 18th-century settlement of the general area by the Franciscan friars. It was a pleasant place to live—warm, but generally kept comfortable by breezes that swept across the mesa from the ocean.

The living area of our house was shaped like a fat letter L, with a covered patio in the corner of the L. From a rafter of the patio hung a ceramic wind chime that my mother had made—a quarter moon with several stars suspended from it—which occasionally clanged pleasantly, if not melodically, in the breeze. Beyond the patio was a small walled garden. Against the back wall, I had planted three bougainvillea plants, which now climbed up trellises. They were gorgeous—a brilliant orange one flanked by two of the traditional fuchsia pink color.

We could look out onto the patio from both the dining room and the family room, and one day, as I glanced out through the sliding glass door of the latter, I saw some pieces of what appeared to be straw stuck in the lower curve of the moon. My puzzlement didn't last long. First one hummingbird and then another flew up and added a few new pieces of dried grass then flew away, soon to return with more. After many such trips, a nest began to take shape. My husband Jim and I were enthralled with their industrious activity.

At work the next day, I couldn't stop wondering what was happening on the patio. When I got home, I went straight to the windows. The nest was complete, and one of the tiny birds, surely the mother-to-be, was ensconced inside it. Soon the other one, presumably the father, arrived to join her, bringing a snack of some sort. I'm not sure whether they took turns sitting in the nest or foraging for food, but one was on egg-warming duty all the time.

Perhaps a couple of weeks passed, with Mama and Papa in attentive attendance. But then we realized that the nest was being left unattended for short periods. Both parents were kept busy foraging for food for their babies. At first, we couldn't see the babies, so deep in the tiny nest they were. We could see only the parents, perched on the side of the nest, lowering their beaks to deposit bits of food into the hungry mouths of the little ones. Were there two, three, or more? We didn't know.

Then one day, we saw tiny beaks sticking up out of the nest. Mama and Papa had to hover above as they dropped minuscule bits of food into the opened beaks. There was no longer room for them to perch on the nest. A few days later, little heads appeared, peeking out of the nest. The babies were growing fast. How long would it be before they could fly? We really didn't want that day to come. The hummingbird family had become a focal point of our lives.

On a sunny Saturday morning, I looked out the window and saw one of the little ones perched on the edge of the nest, seemingly peering at the brilliant orange and pink bougainvillea. Its little wings fluttered, then stopped. This happened several times. And then, after some vigorous fluttering, the tiny hummingbird took flight, straight to the orange flowers where it sat on a branch, its beak reaching into a blossom. After a moment, it flew over to the neighboring pink flowers, where it rested awhile. My heart was fluttering as hard as the tiny bird's wings, and I couldn't take my eyes away from the scene.

Then it happened. The baby went into full flight, up over the wall and away. My eyes filled with tears. I looked back at the nest. Two more little heads were well above the edge. I think they had seen their sibling fly away, but they seemed not quite ready to do the same. As the day passed, they remained in the nest, but they were alone. Mama and Papa stayed away.

I returned to my Saturday chores, occasionally looking out the window. Later in the day, I looked once more and saw no little heads. While I was busy elsewhere, the other two babies had found the courage to fly away. The hummingbird family was gone. Hummingbirds frequented the bougainvillea, but we couldn't tell if they were our little family or not. We left the nest in place, wondering if it would become home to another family, but it remained vacant.

Late in the summer, we decided to take the nest down, carefully detaching it from the curve of the moon. I brought it into the kitchen and took some pictures. The nest fit into the bowl of a soup spoon, and the tiny shell halves barely fit over a pencil eraser.

Fall came. My niece and nephew in Sacramento were in elementary school, and I decided to send these precious mementos of the hummingbird family for them to share with their classmates during 'show and tell'. This show was a real hit!

During a visit years later, I asked my sister if the hummingbird memento box was still there. She said she thought it was on the top shelf of a storage closet, but we looked and couldn't find it. Thank goodness for photos and memories! I still have the half-moon wind chime, but it has never held another nest.

SNOW

Sandra J. S. Stanton

A little snowflake appeared on the Weather Channel report on my iphone earlier this week. It hasn't snowed yet, but more snowflakes have popped up since— for Thursday, Friday, Saturday, and Sunday of the coming week! Well, the Weather Channel must sometimes change its predictions, but surely four snowflakes in a row can't all be wrong.

I'm not the only one to have noticed the snowflakes, and the news has produced complaints and even groans from many friends and neighbors: "I thought we were going to get away with a mild winter." "Who needs to shovel snow!" "Maybe it will melt before it hits the ground." I keep my smile under wraps, since I am clearly in the minority. But my heart sings, because I love snow!

I have always loved snow. My childhood excitement at looking out the window and seeing fluffy, white flakes drifting down to coat the grass and the hedges and cling to the bare tree limbs has never left me. It is beautiful, simply beautiful!

I think back to snow in Chevy Chase, Maryland, where snow days from school were few, but celebrated with glee. The sleds were brought out of the garage and put to use on the neighborhood streets and the few small hills nearby. There was usually enough to make a snowman, even if the yard went back to dull green, since most of its white covering was needed for the winter icon. The dark bare branches of the cherry trees in front of every house on the block sparkled with their coat of snow and ice. It was fun. It was beautiful. And it made my heart sing.

I remember my excitement at the news of moving to Idaho Falls, where I felt sure that snow would fall from November through March. However, the air in Idaho was dry, and snow wasn't as common as I had expected. But when it came, it came hard and heavy, often high enough to make its way over the top of my boots. So what! We could make a snowman without denuding the yard of snow. Of course, there was snow all winter long in the mountains, so many a weekend was devoted to ski trips, including with the high school ski club. The bus trips were almost as much fun as the snowy slopes.

When we were living in Spain in 1969, we and several friends decided to go to Avila for the New Year holiday. We stayed in the Parador de Avila, a national hotel refurbished from a fortressed castle built in the twelfth century. While we were celebrating inside, it had been snowing outside. By the time we looked out a window, a few minutes into the year of 1970, several inches lay on the ground. We bundled up and climbed the ancient steps to the top of the wall, where we looked up at millions of stars in a midnight blue sky. Below us, the fallen snow hid all signs of contemporary civilization. I looked out over the snowy fields in awe at the thought that my view was the same as that of a soldier on guard on that wall hundreds of years earlier.

During a Christmas spent on Cape Cod, where my two brothers and their families hosted the rest of the family for the holiday, many of us stayed in an old rental house. Christmas Eve was mild—at least for winter—but we awoke Christmas morning to a scene of crystal white. It must have snowed most of the night, but by eight, or so, the sun was shining in a blue sky. The air was frigid, however, and the windowpanes were gloriously decorated with intricate frosted designs. Fortunately, we southern Californians had hit the ski shops for winter clothing, so we were prepared to go out in the snow. And my down jacket served double duty—as an extra pillow at night!

Some years later we left San Diego—where we saw snow only from afar, or if we braved the roads up the mountains—heading for a new home in Bend, OR. We arrived on the Fourth of July, in time for a scorcher of a summer, but early January brought us a real snow storm, counted in feet, not inches—almost four of them! Yes, we were snowed in, but we were prepared, so all we had to do was enjoy the beauty of our surroundings. We spent two more winters in Bend, before moving to Bellingham, and every time snow was predicted overnight, I leapt out of bed in the morning and ran to the window to see if snow had fallen while we slept. If I was rewarded, my heart again sang with joy.

On November 2, 2017, right here in Bellingham, WA, I was rewarded again. The snow was measured in inches and it melted the next day, but once more, I had awakened to beauty in my own yard.

On this day in late January 2019, I look forward with excitement to the coming week. Regardless of how few others seem to share my feelings, if the Weather Channel prediction is accurate, snow will make my heart sing, as always.

Stories from a Photograph

Stories written from a photograph
selected by one member.

A TREE

TREE

George Francis Edward

*I*n *Three Days of the Condor* play, CIA analyst Joe Turner (Robert Redford) finds himself seeking refuge from the CIA in Kathy Hale's (Faye Dunaway's) New York City apartment. Turner, taken aback by Hale's black and white pictures of empty park benches and dreary trees, says, "You're funny. You take pictures of empty streets and trees with no leaves on them."

"It's winter," Kathy says.

I never understood black and white photography. Ansel Adams carried his 16-pound Deardorf camera up steep mountain cliffs and shot black and white landscapes. Viewing Adams' photos, I always thought, "Gee, I wonder what color the trees were?"

Mood is important in any artwork, be it audio, visual, or the printed word. The photo of a tree is depressing to me. I want to edit it and add a couple of colorful leaves! Trees by their nature are more beautiful with foliage than when barren.

I recently returned from Costa Rica, where I snapped this photo of a Strangler fig, also called strangler. Tropical figs (genus Ficus) are named for their tendency to grow upon host trees, resulting in the host's death. Strangler figs are common in tropical forests. I saw some stranglers stretching 30 stories in the air; their central core was hollow, where the host tree once stood.

My point is that trees can be beautiful from the outside, but hollow inside. Just like people.

I believe trees show us aspects of life that we often take for granted. Of course, there are young trees—saplings—and old or dead trees. In the rainforest, dead or decaying trees soon become "nurse logs," from which new trees sprout. The forest shows us a cycle of life, which we often miss because we are stuck in time.

One thing I respect in nature is absolute truth. Trees behave according to their genetic code, and you can expect them to do so. Strangler figs strangle because that is what they do. If you expect a strangler fig to renounce its killer tendency, and be civil like other trees, it ain't gonna happen.

Of course, humans are much more complicated than trees in nature. Seemingly sweet people may hurt you, while evil-looking people may favor you with kindness. I have witnessed both. This is one reason why life is so exciting and worth living.

In Costa Rica, there is a plant called the "Poor Man's Umbrella" that can stretch six feet in diameter. The stem, leaves, and seeds can be poisonous if ingested. What good is this plant?

Well, it grows in areas of the forest that have been cleared or otherwise disturbed. The Poor Man's Umbrella protects small saplings and allows them to grow, without being baked by the sun or trampled by passing animals. It provides shelter for the defenseless. Like I say, I respect nature's truth. Think of the Poor Man's Umbrella as the Mother Teresa of plant life.

Dependent on photosynthesis, trees turn to the light. Their roots grow towards the water. Their bark can shield them from fire, like the Redwoods of California.

Trees mock man's mortality. The Great Bristlecone pine has a lifespan of over 5,000 years.

On the other hand, I have seen trees pecked to death by pileated woodpeckers. I had a fir tree that was felled by a huge colony of wasps. They hollowed its core, causing a winter blowdown. Could it be that trees need an element of luck to survive, just like human beings?

One of my favorite songs is "California' Dreamin" by the Mamas and the Papas:

All the leaves are brown
And the sky is gray
I've been for a walk
On a winter's day
I'd be safe and warm
If I was in L.A
California dreamin'
on such a winter's day

This song equates the brown leaves and cold winter with a wish for a safe and warm environment like Los Angeles. Our photo, for which this essay was written, does not show me a promise for warmth or safety. The bleak-looking tree bodes ill. It's like deciding to move from San Diego to Fargo, North Dakota!

Finally, I'll say one more thing about our black and white, dreary-looking tree. While it presents a hopeless image, it is just one stage in the cycle of life. In the spring, I have no doubt that this tree will sprout new buds. The buds will blossom, and fresh green leaves will grow again and wave in the passing breeze. To everything (turn, turn, turn), there is a season (turn, turn, turn). Maybe we will see a springtime photo of this tree when it is flourishing in all its glory.

'Hope springs eternal in nature and in the human breast,' quotes Alexander Pope. This is the reason why I believe that one of the most beautiful trees is the Christmas Tree—the brightest tree, most colorful, and most symbolic of all.

In the same spirit of hope, maybe one day, while I'm still alive, the Seattle Mariners will win the World Series…Nah! Ain't gonna happen.

AN INSPIRATION

Sita C. Amba-Rao

When I saw the picture of the tree, my mind went back sixty-five years, reminding me of a poem that one of my uncles wrote when I got married. The first line of the poem goes something like: *"Under the Tamarind tree, Sitamma was betrothed to Ambarao."*

My husband, CL's family name, and mine, is Chintikindi, which translated means under the tamarind tree. The rest of his name is Lalitha Ambarao. At this point in my life however, the tree inspires my meditation. I am engrossed in calm chanting and spiritual conversation.

I had another thought as I remembered the *tamarind tree*. There was an Indian book from my childhood titled, "Under the Banyan Tree," with two variations. One is about an old man weaving stories through imagination and telling them to an audience, in an open place in the moonlight. His stories cover different themes of hardship, escape, fear and so on. The other book included stories to delight, educate and entertain children on Indian culture and social norms and practices.

The three trees—tamarind, banyan and our tree in the picture are all quite different in their built. A Tamarind tree is quite dense with foliage and fruit. A Banyan tree is a form of fig tree, with large leaves and quite spread out. It has aerial roots from branches hanging down and taking root in the soil, looking like a tree trunk. Whereas our tree appears like a lattice with fewer and more delicate old leaves.

In India, and other south asian countries, the Banyan tree is considered a heavenly tree. *"It is the place where Gods and spirits of deceased ancestors love hanging out."** Our tree has a ghostly appearance, with many arms stretching either way. Yet, it also has a

* Source: Google

welcoming look, with various branches appearing as an extended family, embracing all its members. I imagine, the sun's rays passing through the lattice, appearing to be dancing and gently swaying, forming lovely silhouettes.

Most of all, on a warm, sunny day, I am sitting under the tree in a circle of friends, drinking cool coconut water—Umm

TREE

Sandra J. S. Stanton

*O*h, beautiful tree, your tall trunk towering toward the sky above,
your large limbs reaching upward and outward and even toward the ground below,
their tiny branches entwined like lace against the blue-grey sky;
I would love to know your story.

When did the wee seed that came from who knows where sprout and become the tiny sapling that became you? I wonder how many of your seeds have produced more trees in the forest.

How old were you when those firs that stand on either side of you came into the world? They look like guards standing at the gate of a fairytale castle.

How have you survived the storms and wildfires that could have felled you? Was it chance, or was there something within you that aspired not only to survive but to reach such height?

What have you seen in your lifetime? How many animals have you sheltered from storms? Surely, deer have huddled beneath you, perhaps scratching your bark with their antlers. Hundreds of squirrels must have scampered up and down your trunk and along your branches, and as many or more birds have nested on your limbs.

Have your leafy branches provided shade for summer picnics around your trunk...or are you too deep into the forest for most to come across you? This is hardly a picnic, but it is pleasant to sit on one of your wide, protruding roots with my sandwich and water bottle.

Soon I must make my way back to civilization, though when I think about it, your home in the forest feels more civilized than much of the busy world I live in. I will carry away a picture of you in my mind and the memory of sharing these few moments together.

Thank you, Tree. And live on!

By way of explanation: I talk to many living entities:

Animals, of course, who respond in their way: Our cat, Dollar, is quite adept at letting us know how he feels—a plaintive meow when he is hungry; rubbing my leg if he wants to be petted; happily greeting us from the front window when we return home. I have talked across the hedge to the deer who visit the yard next door; they respond with a long, gentle look. I have scolded spiders that have made their way into the house, as I scooped them up in some container and released them into the back yard.

But not just animals: I apologize to drooping flowers as I give them an overdue drink; their response is to be standing tall by the next morning. I have thanked the apple tree for dropping a beautiful piece of fruit on the hedge, rather than the driveway, injuring its perfect red skin. I have praised trees for their brilliantly colored fall leaves or soft pink spring blossoms.

So, there's nothing surprising about my talking to Tree, if only on paper. If I were to come across him in his forest one day, I think I would recognize him. Then we could have a nice chat.

A TREE

Elizabeth Jane Pryce

*T*his particular tree, stands at the top of the trail leading down into Squalicum Park. I pass it most days when I am out walking the dogs, either in the morning or the evening. But on this particular day, I stopped and looked back. I was suddenly reminded of the ornamental trees one can buy to display cards or pictures!

I turned to continue walking, but turned back again to look at the tree, wondering just why I had that thought. Finding no answer, I shook my head and continued down the trail. I have looked up at that same tree in the wind, rain and snow, each time a very different thought or memory has run though my head.

In the winter when the snow falls, the neighborhood children, gather under the tree with their sleds and sometimes their dogs, to enjoy their school snow day. I remember being there with my two grandchildren one year, two sleds, red and blue. Their job was to climb onto the sled and aim downwards, avoiding the many other children sliding down the hill. My job, was to help drag the sled back up to the tree again! At some point, I left them to their own devices and went back home to fetch hot chocolate and cookies. Now each year when it snows, I watch for the children coming and going and smile at my memories, as the dogs and I slowly move past them at the top of the hill.

There have been a few storms since we moved to Bellingham, and I wonder if and when this tree might break in the wind, or its branches start cracking and falling. I am afraid that they might fall on me or my dogs and that we might be trapped. I move more quickly then, dragging the dogs with me. The winds in my ears hurts, even with my coat pulled tightly around me.

Once, someone reported seeing a cougar in the area. For a long while after that, I found myself looking up in the trees, on the far side of the park, checking for the possibility of the cougar being in one of them; just waiting to pounce and scoop my little dog up in one mouthful. But usually, all I ever saw were noisy crows flying in and out of the trees and squirrels with twitching tails!

In the early spring the sticky buds of the new leaves have a pink bronzed look. The color spreads slowly until the buds unfurl into long, thin, pale green leaves. Once fully formed they are just a plain old green color, with whitish backs, which rustles in the light breezes of the spring and summer seasons.

Every year seems the same and yet vastly different. Many seasons have come and gone. There are more children now than ten years ago. The dogs, I have now, are not the same ones I had, when I first started walking this trail. Even the park itself has changed. When I first came here, the park was a place of business called Pacific Concrete, I took my truck there, to load gravel and sand for my landscaping jobs. There was a big beaver in the stream by the road, my adult children were still children then, playing in the brush and coming home with cuts and bruises. Even the tree has changed, growing taller and wider. Its many spindly sister trees have been cut down, but this one has lived, to become majestic.

JUAN PABLO

JON LUBAUSKI

Sita C. Amba-Rao

$\mathcal{T}$he picture shows a biologist, Jon Lubauski, who was excited to find a sapling of a rare species of an indigenous medicinal plant in the midst of the Amazon forest. The Amazon has a wide variety of plants, shrubs and trees, many of which had medicinal properties and were used by the natives. It would seem like they were begging to be discovered and used. In fact, Lubo (as he was popularly known) learned about this particular species from the natives.

Lubo was there on a special grant from a large pharmaceutical company in the Midwest America. The grant was for exploration and research of plant based medicinal sources, as an alternative treatment to the traditional allopathic drugs, particularly for chronic and difficult-to-treat illnesses. His grant had enabled him to bring a group of his students, as part of the project to learn about the Amazon species. This scientist was very passionate and committed to his study and discovery of those plants, and was eager to stimulate his students' interest. This was evident from the intense manner in which he appears to be explaining the plant to his students.

The team had been searching a long time before finding this plant. Now it would be another long journey home. However, with an equally enthusiastic group of collaborators, Lubo was looking forward to the week, hoping it would be a great adventure! Their daily routine all week would be to wake up at 5 a.m. have a hearty breakfast and be ready to leave their site by 7 a.m. A group of three native men would go with them as their guides. They would drive the jeep to the beginning of the forest, leave it there and trek into the forest for their exploration. The natives would carry their lunch, water and other needed containers for the collection of plants. Around noon the team found a clear patch where they can stop for lunch.

They then took some time relaxing and renewing their energy with entertaining songs by the natives. Their attempts to emulate the natives' singing ended up with laughter. After that it was back to work. Following a long day of search and discussion, they make their way back to the jeep and back to the village.

After cleaning up, they were treated to a sumptuous dinner of fresh roots vegetables, rice and beans. The natives believed in a vegetarian diet, to keep them healthy. After socializing with the natives for a short while, they all retired early to bed. They needed to hit the road at dawn next morning.

THE GREEN MAN

Elizabeth Jane Pryce

*M*y first thought, when I saw this picture was, Oh, a 'Green Man'. He wears green and is surrounded by green.

The 'Green Man' is a mystical figure. In ancient British heritage, he is a forest symbol, a defender of green spaces. He adorns churches and other buildings of Christianity. He has been found in ancient Roman and Greek cultures. He is a pagan artifact derived from the ancient Celts' worship of the head, which they considered the seat of the soul. He is the archetypal symbol of nature that influences and inspires cultures around the world.

Suddenly my mind was racing; I was back in1989, in Cambridge, England, working on my teaching certificate. I went in search of the mythical, medieval story I wrote about a peasant girl, *Gentillese*.

The story opened with the heroine, sad and all alone after burying her parents. She must now seek her fortune elsewhere. Wandering, she becomes lost in the dark forest, where she falls asleep. She is startled awake by a man, half way between the ordinary world and the wildness of nature. The "Green Man" reassures her and gives her his counsel, along with a magical cloak.

As in all fairytales, there is an evil sorceress. In this story, she is a shifting shape of undefined form, yearning to capture a soul and enter the world of mankind. To this end she is using her powers to entice a noble knight who has also become lost, wandering in the same forest as the girl. When Gentillese enters the same clearing as the knight, a breath of spring air parts the forest gloom for a second.

There is a whirling of dark, cold air, followed by a cry of anguish. The cloak of truth saves Gentillese but the knight lies dying, wounded by the thorns of desire. Gentillese gently covers the knight with her cloak, her hot tears falling onto his face. He opens his eyes, "Sweet lady, you have saved me. I will pledge my heart to you in honest faith, yet I am pierced with a poison dart, which with false fire draws my life away."

The story continues with the "Green Man" appearing again, sending Gentillese on a quest that will save the noble knight's life. "A rose grows deep in a garden torn from the soil of rich loam, find the knight sprung completely of flowers and the cloak's truth will you find, to light your way home."

The purpose of writing this story was to experience and use all the audio-visual-linguistic resources available in the department; staging, lighting and costume. We were encouraged to work as a group, as we might in the future, encourage our pupils to do. Our lecturer gave us the title, "Looking up in Cambridge," as a motivational idea to find hidden themes of mystery, outside of the usual tourist perspective.

The work, leading up to the project was fun, but also very stressful for me. I lived a double life in those days. During the week, Monday morning to Friday afternoon, I was a student renting a room in Cambridge and living activity-filled days and evenings. It was my dream life! On Friday afternoons after classes, I would catch the train back into London for the weekend where my primary life was, my three children, a dog, two cats, and childcare provider—whom I found out was incapable of taking care of himself, let alone three children!

In the two days I was home, I cleaned, cooked meals for everyone for the coming week, and occasionally entertained some of my friends, from earlier college days, when the children went to visit their father for the weekend.

My only real time with my children was in the evenings, watching TV, reading stories and checking up on homework. Looking back, the children were incredible, especially my daughter who was the oldest, at only thirteen. But so much can fall through the cracks when a mother is not there for her children. All the responsibility of the week fell to my daughter, even to looking after the childcare provider, who couldn't even wash his long hair without help!

No one in my family, not even the children's father, knew the whole story of my double life. Most of them believed I travelled back and forth each day, but the expense of that would have been prohibitive. I believe my rent was about twenty-five pounds for the week, and the train fare would have been in the hundreds for a month's pass. Plus, I would have had to leave around six in the mornings and not return until eight in the evenings!

Most of the students in the class were in their twenties, having come straight from college. I was by that time in my forties. I don't think I would have made it, if it hadn't been for Christy, the gay man I rented the room from. He was, my mystical, gentle, "Green Man," who opened my eyes to so many truths.

JUAN PABLO SABORIO

George Francis Edward

*O*ur wonderful Costa Rican guide, Juan Pablo, revealed to us that he answered to many names—Juan, Pablo, or "J.P." Dana and I decided to call him "J.P."

We met J.P. at the Doubletree Hotel. He introduced himself on the first day of our Collette Tour, telling us that he had worked as a Tour Manager with Collette for nineteen years! He also said he was the father of three beautiful children, and "happily" divorced, which caused a big laugh from the group.

J.P. was a keen observer of nature—both human and animal. He also had a keen interest in his country. He told us stories about the American mercenary, William Walker (1824 – 1860), and how Walker attempted to make Costa Rica a southern slave state of the United States. Walker was defeated by native Costa Ricans in the Battle of Rivas in 1856.

J.P. described to us the habits of native animals, fish, and birds. He was extraordinarily well-versed in ornithology (study of birds), herpetology (study of reptiles and amphibians) and primatology (study of monkeys). I marveled at how he could identify a bird by its song.

As much as J.P. knew his fauna, he seemed to know flora even more. J.P.described an epiphyte in the photo as "the smartest and most independent plant" known to man. It "derives its moisture and nutrients from the air, rain, water (in marine environments) or from debris accumulating around it" (Wikipedia). In other words, this plant can grow anywhere, and it is not dependent on another plant for nourishment. Epiphytes can grow on tin roofs.

On the other hand, many trees and plants in the rain forest are symbiotic. One example is the acacia tree, which allows a type of ant to live in its hollow thorns and feed from the tree. In return, the ants provide protection against herbivores (like

Strangler figs) and keep the ground around this tree clear of other plants that would compete for sunlight, water and nutrients.

Another symbiotic relationship, involves Azteca ants. The ants protect the Cecropia trees against grazing herbivores and strangling vines. In exchange, the Cecropia provides shelter for the ants as well as nourishment from the underside of its leaves.

J.P. allowed a bullet ant to climb a stick he was holding so we could see it. This ant can grow to over one inch long, it is also called the "big black ant." Bullet ants punish an adversary with one of the most painful insect stings known in Costa Rica. J.P. told us that if you are bitten by a bullet ant, you will never forget it!

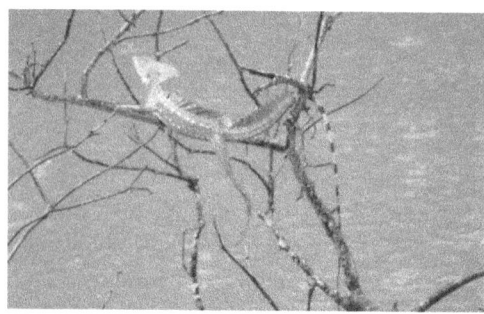

Jesus Christ Lizard

To give an example of J.P.'s expertise on reptile behavior; we came across a amphibian called a 'Jesus Christ lizard' because it literally walks on water. J.P. told us to focus our cameras on the lizard "because it is getting ready to walk on water." Sure enough, right after he alerted us it ran across the river. Right on cue!

We asked J.P. how he knew the lizard was going to walk. First, J.P. said the lizard was acting nervous, he could tell it wanted to get away from our tour boat. Secondly, the lizard had descended from its perch in the tree branches, to the water's edge, it was preparing to run across the river. Makes perfect sense!

In short, years of observation and study have given J.P. unbelievable insight into animal behavior and the complex ecosystem of the rain forest! He was born to be a travel guide. We were very fortunate to have him as our guide.

THE PIANIST

THE PIANIST

Elizabeth Jane Pryce

*A*s a young teenager, I remember how difficult it was to do research for any project. The information was so incomplete! Now, although being a partial technophobe, what I love about the internet, is having the access to more information than I could possibly absorb in a lifetime!

Receiving the photo of a pianist, without any other information piqued my interest. Who was he? Where should I begin? I thought that it probably came from the internet. I started my search with famous pianists; there were a great number, ranging from ancient to very modern, and of all ages. Next I searched the style of clothes, to try and determine the decade. I searched for famous pianists in the 1900s. I continued to scroll, (a word, dating back to early parchment writings. Its uses were limited after the early middle ages, but it reappeared with the advent of computers!) The next search brought me to the "25 best piano players of all time," which was based on a question put to the Classic FM Presenters, who after a heated debate, made the list. I scrolled down. At first I thought the photo was of Vladimir Ashkenazy, but although the piano and position were similar, the pianist's hairline was wrong. Finally I came to Vladimir Horowitz! The search said, *There was a strong case for Vladimir Horowitz to be crowned the greatest pianist of all time.* Success, I was happy!

Vladimir lived from 1903 to 1989. He was born in Kiev, Ukraine, then part of the Russian Empire. He made his debut in 1920 in a solo recital. In 1925 he emigrated to the West, ostensibly to study under Artur Schnabel in Berlin, but Vladimir had planned never to return. He had stuffed as much American dollars and British currency, as was possible, into his shoes!

He gave his debut performance in Carnegie Hall in 1928, playing Tchaikovsky's Piano Concerto No 1. He went on to become an American citizen, best known for his performances of romantic works, including Chopin, Rachmaninov and Schumann. Vladimir Horowitz returned to the Soviet Union for the first time in 1986, playing in Moscow and Leningrad; the significance was as much political as musical. After returning to the States, he received the Presidential Medal of Freedom, from president Ronald Reagan.

Although he continued to record music until he died, his final recital was in Germany in June 1987. He died of a heart attack in November 1989 in New York City, at the age of 86.

For this, and many other kinds of research I have done, I am very thankful for the internet and for having a computer. One of the quotes I found from Vladimir Horowitz, fits him nicely, "Never be afraid to dare."

BARRY HOWARD

George Francis Edward

Our writing assignment is on Vladimir Horowitz—the Russian-born, classical pianist. I know nothing of Horowitz or classical music, so I will quickly change the subject to somebody I knew and loved, Barry Horowitz. Barry told me his family changed their surname to Howard.

Barry and I roomed together as college undergraduates. Sadly, Barry died last March 22nd at the age of sixty-nine. I learned of Barry's passing in our alumni publication, The Pennsylvania Gazette.

Please allow me to share some of my favorite Barry memories with you.

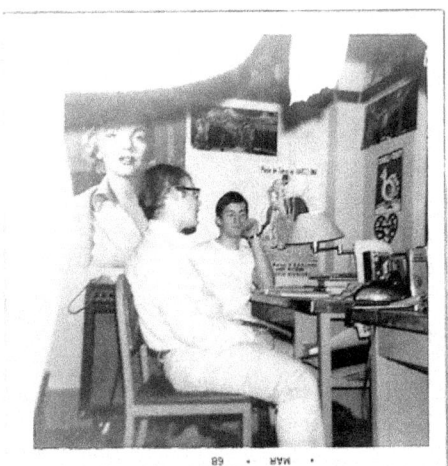

Barry and George

As freshmen, Barry roomed at 108 Ashhurst, next door to me. Barry's roommate, Michael, was a party animal, and occasionally—a "fall down drunk." When drunk, he called everybody "Skippy." Seriously! Campus cops, friends, strangers—Michael called everyone Skippy. Barry and Michael were completely different.

At Ashhurst, Barry and I seemed to hit it off, and he would wander into my dorm room at any time of the day or night to educate me on a host of topics. Barry was so well-read and knowledgeable, that he became my "go to" guy whenever I wanted to know anything about Economics, Finance, Chemistry, or even"why the sky was blue."

If it hadn't been for Barry, I doubt I would have graduated from the Wharton School.

Barry had an answer for all of my questions, no matter how complex the subject. On the other hand, not once did Barry tell me my question was elementary, and not once did Barry stare at me and say, "I can't believe you don't know that!" Not once.

Of course, I made fun of Barry. He pronounced his name like "Berry" so that is what I called him. Barry pronounced 'bury,' 'berry' and 'Barry' the same. It was weird!

It was a turning point in my life when Barry and I decided to room together as sophomores in 443 Hopkinson Dorm (photo at left). Were it not for Barry's acceptance to the London School of Economics, we might have roomed together as juniors.

I was incredibly fortunate to have a wonderful guy like Barry, make a roommate commitment to me for an entire year.

Our relationship was beautiful, without any stress. I don't remember a single argument. I think we viewed each other as brothers, and trusted each other as only brothers can.

I believe Barry's father was a Cleveland cop. Barry and I were like two police partners riding in the same squad car. Each had the other's back... Barry protected me, and I tried to do the same for him.

I recall that Barry had an unnatural, crazy addiction for "tuna hoagies;" he would eat one almost every day. I teased him mercilessly about his food choices. After all, who could eat a tuna hoagie seven days a week?

I remember when Barry mentioned his girlfriend "Elayne," he immediately turned happy and joyful. I think he loved Elayne more than tuna hoagies—which, believe me, was saying something.

After graduation, Barry and Elayne married, she remained by his side until the day he died.

Barry went on to accomplish great things. He was accepted at Harvard Law School but turned Harvard down because the University of Chicago Law School offered him a full scholarship. Some time later, I asked Barry what he did for a living, and he told me "international law." He explained that sometimes, he purchased islands for his clients. Barry was Executive Vice President and Chief Compliance Officer at Equus Capital Partners and real estate advisor to the University of Pennsylvania Endowment Fund.

Barry's obituary stated that Barry was known for… *"efforts to wisely guide the lives of young people;"* and even though he was of the Jewish faith, he was a proud member of the Board of Roman Catholic High School.

As one of those young people who benefitted from Barry's kindness and guidance, I cannot think of my undergraduate years at Penn without reflecting on Barry. Just thinking of him makes me smile, his acts of kindness, humor, and wisdom, which he shared with me on a daily basis. If I close my eyes, I still can hear his voice.

I am eternally grateful to have known him.

On the other hand, I can't recall meeting Vladimir Horowitz…

THE PIANIST

Sita C. Ambra-Rao

*W*hen I saw the picture of the pianist, I thought I could not write anything about it except to observe that the pianist seemed intense, playing his favorite instrument. It appeared that one of his fingers was short, I thought that he must be a great pianist, as it was my friend Joan, who sent the picture. She loves classical music.

Over the Thanksgiving holiday, I was visiting a niece. We watched a movie from India, titled "Sarvam Thalamayam," meaning the Omnipresence of Rhythm, or everything is filled with rhythm. Then the following Friday, I heard one of our writing group members read her piece on the subject. She informed us that the picture was of Vladimir Horowitz, the famous Russian-American pianist. She had searched the web for his story, and concluded her piece with one of his very impressive quotes, *"Never be afraid to dare."* My mind clicked.

The movie I saw about 'Omnipresence of Rhythm' had a similar underlying theme: taking risks and daring to break barriers in music. That inspired me into delving further into the connection. The protagonist in the movie impassioned by music tells his girlfriend, *"My life, heart and body are all beating in rhythm."* Then I thought, Aha! why don't I integrate both the themes and write about it.

In the movie, a low caste Christian young man, Peter was obsessed with the desire to learn to play the percussion instrument, Mridangam or mrdangam, a two headed drum made of wood in barrel shape with sheep skin embedded on either side. In south Indian classical music the mridangam is played to accompany the vocal artist.

There is a caste tension underlying the musicians and players, which is guarded closely and perpetuated zealously. Peter's father is a craftsman who builds this instrument and supplies it to an acclaimed mridangist, but never considers playing it himself. Peter breaks this barrier, and persuades the musician, Vembu, to teach him to play, despite his father's discouragement and the insults of Vembu's assistant. Due to these adverse circumstances Peter is turned away by Vembu.

Peter leaves in despair, He travels all over India on his quest to learn to play. He discovers various forms of musical instruments and returns home healed. Peter takes a chance to prove his new creative talent in a contest and succeeds. Vembu sees this and is initially disappointed that his star student had deviated from his traditional, sacred learning to what he calls a "diluted" art.

But he soon realizes his folly and recognizes the magic of adaptive and innovative music. He admits as much to Peter, as the latter apologizes for having moved away from the revered pure classical music.

But Vembu praises him for his accomplishment, blesses him, and passes on his own long held title. He explains that classical music is not static like water in a well. He describes it as a continuously flowing river, which integrates itself, like falling raindrops into the rivers. In turn, the rivers flows into the ocean, like the music, creating a great transformation.

A MAN IN WHITE

DOWN THE MISSISSIPPI

Sandra J. S. Stanton

$\mathcal{O}$n a warm afternoon in June 1957, Camilla and Andrea Shephart boarded the *Delta Queen* in Memphis, Tennessee. Their morning had been spent touring that well-known Mississippi River port city, oohing and aahing as they drove past beautiful parks and palatial mansions, many built well before the Civil War. Now, the two cousins were even more excited at the thought of their week-long cruise on this historical paddlewheel steamboat, on the river since 1927. The entire ship had been recently refurbished, and when they entered their cabin, they were thrilled to find it elegantly furnished in carved mahogany, with white crocheted spreads on the twin beds. Wrought iron chairs graced the small balcony.

After unpacking their bags, they spent some time deciding what to wear to their first dinner on board. Before dinner, however, the girls (well, age 22) were going to the lounge, where their older cousin Bobby would be playing the piano. He would be their escort on the trip. To tell the truth, their parents wouldn't have arranged this "college graduation present" if Bobby weren't going to be with them.

About 5:30 p.m., Camilla in an ivory silk sheath and Andie in a full-skirted turquoise brocade dress locked the door of their cabin and headed to the lounge. At the entrance to the Queen's Lounge, an easel supported a poster. Under a super picture of their cousin at the piano, sporting a white suit with a black tie and pocket square, a caption announced that "Bobby Shephart, renowned lounge pianist of Chicago and New York City, will be playing every afternoon and evening for your listening and dancing pleasure. Please join him from 3:00 to 6:00 and then from 8:30 to 11:30 or so.

As his cousins walked in, Bobby lifted a hand from the keyboard to give them a wave and then motioned them toward a reserved table near the piano. Two minutes after they sat down, a waiter arrived with a bottle of champagne and three flutes. When Bobby finished that number, he stood up and introduced Andrea and Camilla to the audience and excused himself for a few minutes to join them at the table. After big hugs, he filled two flutes and poured a sip into one for himself, then proposed a toast to "three cousins heading down the Mississippi!" Hearing him, the audience joined in the toast. Then Bobby returned to the piano for a closing number. The audience applauded and rose to leave, waving to the cousins on their way out.

Bobby's hours conveniently allowed him to dine with his cousins at 6:30, so they made their way to the dining room. Soon after they were seated, a couple of fellows who had been in the lounge approached, introduced themselves as Rick McDonald and Leo Collins, and asked if they could join the cousins. "Sure, glad to have you," Bobby said. "What brings you aboard the *Delta Queen?*"

Rick explained, "Well, we both work at George Engineering in Memphis, just a few blocks from the wharf, and we've watched enviously as other people have boarded this ship. So, when we were asked to attend a conference in New Orleans, we decided to try it ourselves, rather than just take the train."

Leo added, "Absolutely! We both have vacation days and decided to use them to make this trip. I've wanted to take a cruise ever since I watched people boarding ships in Boston, my hometown.

Bobby said, "This is the first time I've played on a cruise ship. It's a nice change from playing the same clubs, night after night. And, instead of paying the cruise fare, I get paid to play!" They all laughed. Bobby thought to himself, 'I think they liked my music, but I believe they're more interested in Andie and Camilla than me. I'll bet we see them in the lounge this evening.'

After a leisurely and delicious Cajun-style dinner, with plenty of lively conversation, the cousins excused themselves to take a turn around the deck before returning to the lounge. Sure enough, no more than fifteen minutes after Bobby began to play at 8:30, in walked Rick and Leo. They waved to the girls, but, playing it cool, they went up to the bar and had a beer. Then they asked the waiter to take two champagne cocktails to Camilla and Andie. Surprised, the girls told the waiter to ask the two gentlemen to join them—just the scenario Rick and Leo had hoped for, and Bobby had expected!

Leo was two inches taller than Rick, and Camilla a bit taller than Andie, so that's how they paired up to dance, although they politely switched partners from time to time. After dancing several numbers, they returned to their table. They made a great conversational foursome, finding they shared many interests, including the history of the South, especially the Civil War era. Camilla was the only one born in the South—in Mississippi. Andie hailed from southern California, but her parents were Mississippians. The girls explained about the cruise being a college graduation present from their parents, who wanted them to learn more about their roots in the South. Leo laughed as he said, "So I'm the only foreigner—born in Toronto, but I grew up in the Midwest and went to Wisconsin State." They were an eclectic bunch, for sure.

Then Rick piped up, "It seems we're all interested in going ashore in some of the port towns where the *Queen* stops. I know they offer tours, but they're not cheap. What would you all think about creating our own tours?" Smiles all around indicated a definite yes. Bobby came to the table when he took a break, and they told him of their plans. "Great idea," he said with a grin. "You'll see just what you want for a lot less money. But be sure you plan carefully and are back on board well before the ship sails. The captain won't wait for anybody. I'd like to join you when I can, though of course I'm in the lounge every afternoon and, since I play until midnight, I need to sleep in. Well, back to the piano."

Camilla, with her knowledge of Mississippi, made a few suggestions about their 'tours'. "Vicksburg, founded in 1811, and Natchez, in 1716 probably have the most to offer. In between the main ports of call, we can see a lot from the ship, and we can debark at smaller stops if we want. We have a few days to work out our tours. There are some brochures in the lobby that will help. I'll get some tomorrow morning, and perhaps we can make some plans after lunch."

"Okay," Leo said, "but now, let's dance!" Bobby was happy to see them out on the floor and played a whole medley of swing music. Then he switched to ballads, some of which he sang as he played. The four 'tourists' were ready for a little slow dancing by that time. About 10:30, Andie and Camilla told their new friends goodnight, then stopped by the piano to thank Bobby for a great evening of music and company. He winked at them as they left. Rick and Leo stayed for a final beer.

Over the next few days, in addition to putting together their tours in Vicksburg and Natchez, the foursome enjoyed life aboard the *Delta Queen*. Rick and Leo hit the gym every morning. Andie and Camilla went on a tour of the ship, joined in a class on Creole and Cajun cooking, and spent hours on deck, just looking at the small towns and farmlands they passed, sometimes joined by Leo and Rick. On occasion, the girls sat on their own deck.

The foursome's evenings were usually spent together—often with Bobby at dinner and in the lounge. When they arrived in Vicksburg, they were ready for their first tour of this elegant and hospitable city. Bobby met them for lunch in town and for part of their afternoon tour. They all walked back to the wharf, where Andie snapped a picture of their handsome, nattily dressed cousin before he boarded, just in time to get to the lounge. The foursome resumed their tour, which for the girls included a little shopping. Then, back to the Queen, well before she pulled away from the wharf.

Two days later, they reached Natchez. Tour plans in hand, the foursome headed ashore, but this time they split up, visiting special sites that each couple had chosen, with plans to meet at a café at 3:00. Rick and Andie were early and sat down on a bench to wait for Leo and Camilla. Suddenly a man rushed up behind them, grabbed Andie's purse, and ran down the nearby alley! She screamed, and Rick was up in a flash, running after the purse snatcher. But as he passed by a trash bin in the alley, he was tackled by a second man, knocking him flat on his face. Andie caught up with Rick and saw the second man run down the alley after his partner in crime. Both men turned left at the next street.

About that time, Leo and Camilla arrived on the scene. The foursome quickly assessed the situation. Leo returned to the ship to tell the captain. Camilla insisted on staying with Andie and Rick. They went into the café, and Rick called the police, who told them to come to the station and file a report. Rick's leg was bleeding, and he was limping, so they took a taxi. Meeting with the police would take some time, and the ship was due to depart at 5:00.

While they were waiting to meet with a detective, Leo called the police department and talked to Rick. "I went to the lounge first and told Bobby what happened. He was horrified and excused himself to the audience to take me to the captain's quarters, where I am now. Bobby, of course, had to return to the lounge. Captain Merrick is very concerned about us, but the ship must leave on schedule. However, he has given me instructions about what we should do. I'm not leaving you three! I'll be at the police department shortly.

"The captain said that as soon as we're through at the police department, you should go to an emergency clinic nearby and have your injuries cared for. He gave me the telephone number of the St. Francisville Inn and told me to book rooms for us tonight. There's a bus station near the clinic, from where we can take an express bus that will stop right at the hotel. It's not that far. The Queen will arrive during the night and is scheduled to remain until noon. We can board in time for breakfast, if we like, but the captain insists on meeting with us in the morning to get a full account of the incident for the company... Okay, I'm on my way to join you."

The detective helped Rick file the complaint and had a police car take them to the clinic. The cut on Rick's leg required five stitches, and some bruises were developing, so the doctor gave him crutches to keep the weight off that leg. The foursome got to the bus station just in time to board the express at 6:30. By 8:00, they were checking into the hotel. The desk clerk said that Captain Merrick had called and told him to send the bill for their rooms and their dinner to the Queen. They couldn't believe how well they were being treated by everyone!

Seeing the Queen at the wharf the next morning brought smiles to their faces. They boarded right at 8:00 and went to their rooms to shower and change clothes—not easy for Rick! Then he and Leo joined the girls for breakfast, after which they met with Captain Merrick and told him every detail about their unhappy incident and thanked him for his help. He invited them to join him for dinner that night, bringing Bobby with them.

When the five of them approached the captain's table that evening, he motioned for Andie to take the seat next to him. Rick pulled out her chair, but as Andie looked down, she cried, "My purse! How...?"

Captain Merrick, with a sly smile on his face, explained. "Sometime after our meeting this morning, a Natchez policeman delivered it, but unfortunately I wasn't informed. It seems that a couple in Natchez had seen two men rifling through a woman's purse last evening. They pulled out some money and then tossed away the purse. The couple picked it up and called the police, who arrived in no time flat. They got a description of the men and took the purse—your purse, Andie—back to the station. Since the Queen had left, they decided to send a policeman to St. Francisville to return it. When a contrite desk clerk finally brought it to me an hour ago, you didn't answer your cabin phone, so I decided to surprise you. It's too bad you lost your money, but at least you have your purse and everything else of importance in it."

"Oh, I don't care about the money. There wasn't much left in my purse anyway—after I bought the dress I'm wearing this evening. The shop had it delivered to the ship." All present noted that the beautiful green silk dress just matched Andie's eyes. It was an excellent purchase. The captain declared it to be a fortuitous purchase as well, since Andie had bought it with money that would otherwise have been stolen. Then they all lifted their waiting flutes of champagne in a toast to Andie's good luck.

The foursome stayed on board for the rest of the trip to New Orleans, where they debarked after goodbyes to all their new friends, as well as Bobby, who would continue playing on the Queen's return trip up the Mississippi. The engineering conference wasn't to begin until the next day, which was also when the girls had flights home. So, they made the most of their last day together seeing everything as they could of New Orleans without too much walking for Rick. They visited Jackson Square and then took a bus tour of some of New Orleans' awesome mansions, eclectically built in Greek, Italian, and Victorian styles. Last on the tour was the city's famous cemetery commonly known as The City of the Dead. That evening, a visit to the French Quarter ended with dinner at the legendary Court of Two Sisters, where they enjoyed a sumptuous Creole dinner and some great New Orleans jazz.

While the two couples had originally paired up according to height while dancing in the Queen's Lounge, by the end of their second day together, they had clicked as paired—Camilla with Leo, and Andie with Rick—and their relationships seemed destined to last beyond their adventures on the Delta Queen. Before they parted after breakfast the following morning, they shared addresses and phone numbers and then found themselves thinking of sharing another travel adventure together.

I WAS A DREAMER

Elizabeth Jane Pryce

J was a good looking young man back then. I was getting ready to leave for the dream of my life; was always looking for something special just over the horizon! I never saw the sea before I was posted to Royal Sussex Regiment as a corporal in the Great War.

Blimey, I'll never forget the night I got the search light stuck and I watched a Jerry drop his bomb right down the light shift! I was mesmerized, but Tommy, he was a good mate, he gave the warning and we all scattered. I lost a few days pay after that shindig! We survived that night, but Tommy didn't survive the war. He got shot down over France. So many blokes never came home. There wasn't much to come back to either.

That's why I'm standing by the ship. I was getting ready to leave for a new life in Australia, but I did a silly thing when I collected my army pay. I was on my way up to London, when it was pinched out of my back pocket. Edie, she was so mad at me, but she was a good sport and stood by me. We had to work our passage out to Australia as steward and stewardess. Unfortunately, we could not go on the same ship. Crew were not allowed to be married.

I had met my wife, Edith, because of Peter, my brother. He was returning to England, after the war, to see our family and meet his wife Winifred's family. Both Edith and

I went to meet them at the docks, and fell in love! My poor Edie, she never knew how much she would have to put up with! Once back in Australia, Peter had written me about the Returned Soldiers Settlement Act. He thought we would be eligible to apply for Crown Lands in Leeton, New South Wales. We could build our farms next to each other.

Unfortunately, Peter had made a mistake. The land was only offered to soldiers who had fought as Imperial soldiers! He had, but I was a British soldier. None of this did we find out until we were already in Australia! Those first years were very difficult. We had to rely on the mercies of Peter and Winifred, something Eddie found very distasteful! But I digress, the journey first. It was hard work, but what an experience! The steamer was built for the Orient Line in 1918 and was the first passenger steamer to go to Australia after the war!

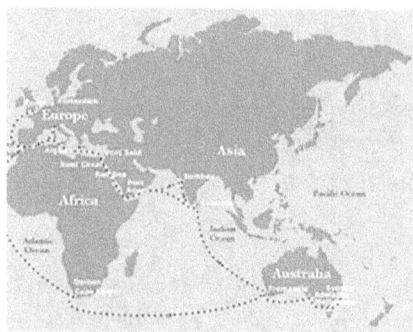

We left Tilbury, London, in November 1919, stopping at Gibraltar, Naples and Port Said, then went through the Suez Canal. Oh my, that was something! Only one ship could fit at a time and everyone was on deck, watching with their hearts in their mouths hoping we wouldn't bump into the sides. It really felt like we could have taken a step off the ship right onto the land! We then steamed on through the Red Sea to Port Aden, and then across to Ceylon. After that, we across the Indian Ocean to Fremantle, Melbourne and finally Sydney, where I disembarked. The whole journey took weeks, but at least I didn't have to do my own washing! I remember, when Peter went out to Australia, he wrote home that he had to do all his own washing and cooking. He had gone out on one of the old sailing ships.

I didn't go ashore much, as I was trying to save every penny I had. Of course other crew members did, and shared their stories, plus, I overheard much of the gossip from the passengers. "Stopovers" were a practical necessity in those days, refueling, a need for fresh food and water, as well as the unloading and picking up of passengers. It was a time for short adventures, souvenirs and sights and sounds most people had never seen before.

The passengers and occasionally the crew, when not busy, were able to play some of the games provided on board. They had Quoits, shuttlecock and ping-pong. My favorite was ping-pong. I became quite good; and later, in Australia, played in a few table-tennis tournaments, as it became called.

On the final leg of the journey across the Indian Ocean, we had a wonderful celebration crossing the Equator. Everyone was involved. The origins of the ceremony goes back to ancient times, when sailors were very superstitious and mades their pleas to the god Neptune to bring them safely home. There was a lot of dressing up and hilarity. I wrote home to let Edie know what to expect when she came out. Everyone on board received a *Neptune, King of the Seas*, certificate, because it was our first time crossing the Equator. Years later we would cross it again, going out to visit my sister in the British West Indies. That time, our children received certificates.

Every port in Australia was crowded when we docked, bands playing "Waltzing Matilda," and colorful streamers flying through the air. Passengers and onshore crowds alike were shouting, laughing and crying as they searched the crowds for waiting and arriving families and friends. It took awhile to get through customs officials and baggage handlers before I found Peter. He was waiting for me with a horse and buggy. We had a long way to go over rough country, but I was there, eager to start a new and prosperous way of life!

WHO IS THE MAN IN THE WHITE SUIT?

Sita C. Amba-Rao

Who is the man in the white suit, in the picture? Hmm! This picture took me down memory lane. In my prime, the casual-formal dress for men was all white, mostly both trousers (as pants were known) and shirts. Back then, those on the tennis court wore white as well.

I remember the picture I have of my husband CL on a tennis court hitting a ball with all his strength, it seemed. Also the photo he had of Lord and Lady Mountbatten, the then Viceroy of India, perhaps the last British administrator before India received independence in 1947. He was in all white. With these images floating in my mind, when I saw the picture of the man in white, I thought of a tennis club President standing near an invisible tennis court, with a smile perhaps because of his winning team and about to be interviewed by some eager reporter.

On a second viewing, however, the background appeared to be that of cruise ship? There was an upper passenger deck and circular windows down below. So, he could possibly be the ship's captain, or its director of activities. He could also be posing for a passenger, with an inviting smile.

Other thoughts came to my mind, could he be a smooth talking salesman? Or, maybe he is a potential suitor to a woman, whom he is trying to woo with a pleasant smile and a smart looking outfit?

Whoever it is, I submit to the photographers among us, from our writers' group, to enlighten and entertain us with this mystery. But—one last guess, could he be the photographer who recently went on a Costa Rican vacation with his vibrant wife? While on the cruise did he take this picture of one of that ship's officers? What would you say, George Francis Edward?

UNCLE ART

George Francis Edward

I don't know much about Arthur Haag. I met him sometime in 1977 and he died two years later. When I met Mr. Haag, he was in failing health, partially blind and in his eighties. His nose was red, enlarged and inflamed, likely due to rosacea. He asked us to call him "Uncle Art."

My roommate, Greg, and I met Uncle Art when we moved into our second floor apartment on Hornblend Street in Pacific Beach. Uncle Art lived in the one-bedroom apartment next door. I have no idea how long he lived in Pacific Beach.

If I walked up the steps to my apartment, many times I could hear swing music of the 1950s coming from Uncle Art's open door. When Uncle Art heard our steps, he would stick his head out the door and say hello. He often cracked funny jokes.

To my knowledge, Uncle Art had no surviving relatives, and from what I could see, precious few friends. Greg and I became his surrogate family. If Uncle Art needed something from the store, we would help him as best we could.

Uncle Art was very frail, and he fell down often. Several times Greg or I returned home to discover Uncle Art lying on the floor of his apartment. We called 9-1-1 and paramedics took him to the hospital. Uncle Art would stay in the hospital for a week or so, and then he would be discharged. He would take a yellow cab back to his Pacific Beach apartment.

One time I remember him pasting a sign on his door announcing his return from the hospital. It read "I'M BACK IN THE OLD CORRAL!—UNCLE ART"

Uncle Art had a wonderful sense of humor, considering that he was slowly dying of some type of congestive lung disease. He was a smoker, a chain smoker in fact. He probably started smoking at an early age. The photo was taken at a waterfront pier, with a cruise liner in the background. I assume Uncle Art worked on this ship. Since I knew he worked as an entertainer on cruise ships, sailing around the world.

I think he performed magic tricks and sleight of hand. He showed Greg and me a couple of card tricks, but I don't recall any of them being spectacular. Unlike David Copperfield's famous trick, *"Vanishing the Statue of Liberty."* Uncle Art probably worked the cruise lounges, performing disappearing coin tricks and other illusions.

Uncle Art gave me the photo of him wearing the white Panama suit. When he presented it to me, he mentioned how much he loved performing in front of the passengers. From what I gathered he was a veteran magician for decades. He also mentioned that he was a platinum card member of Continental Airlines. I think this entitled Uncle Art to fly virtually free anywhere in the United States.

Over the course of the two years we knew Uncle Art, he must have entered Mission Bay Hospital half a dozen times. Each one of his visits was at least a week. I seem to recall that once, he was gone at least two weeks. Greg and I would pick up Uncle Art's mail and newspaper when he was in the hospital.

One day we were told by the apartment manager that Uncle Art wasn't coming back to his apartment. He had passed away in Mission Bay Hospital. Just like that, Uncle Art passed from our life. There was no obituary, and I have no idea how the burial arrangements were handled. Uncle Art never confided in us what his plans were *if* or *when* he didn't return to "the old corral" from Mission Bay Hospital. My story can be summed up like this: a lonely, old, blind man died one day in Pacific Beach.

Of course, the wobbling world did not notice, indeed, every one's life continued just as normal. Uncle Art was a magician, but he could not escape this life.

1930s Summer Suits

He was a kind man, and a good man. I wish I had met him aboard his cruise ship, when he was in the prime of his life—strutting around in his white Panama suit, with a jaunty pocket square, and fancy gold watch. I would have enjoyed his companionship, and his wit. I have no doubt that Uncle Art flashed energy and *joie de vivre* during his magical career.

Famed author F. Scott Fitzgerald's tombstone reads "So we beat on, boats against the current, borne back ceaselessly into the past."

Come what may, time is illusive.

I'd like to think Uncle Art, my old blind friend, performed one last illusion—tricking fate with a sleight of hand and returning to his former glory on the high seas.

THE NATIVITY SCENE

NATIVITY SCENE

Sita C. Amba-Rao

*T*he picture of the Nativity scene reminded me of the clay figurines made in India by handicraft artisans. The picture shows Mary and Joseph near the baby Christ; angels and the three wise men coming together to bless and celebrate the birth of Christ. Celebrating Christmas has its commercial, glittery, extravagant spending and gifting aspects. But there is also the spiritual and ritualistic aspect. These thoughts took me back to the celebration of Christmas in India.

When I was young we lived a few years in Kerala, the state with a curious combination of Catholicism with a communist government. At that age I did not pay much attention. But in later years, reading about the celebration of Christmas in India, I realized how wonderfully the occasion was celebrated. Kerala, in the Southwest part of India and a few regions in the Northeast part of India, near Kolkata are the major Christian areas in India.

Christianity was introduced in India with St. Thomas, an apostle from the first century. In Goa, further north it started with the Portuguese occupation. Fast forward and Christmas became Indianized, with an emphasis on food and community.

After independence, as a secular state, India officially declared the religious holidays of Christmas, Good Friday and Easter as national holidays. There was a cultural diffusion, whereby both Christians and non-Christians connected and celebrated together. They wished each other "Subh Krisamas," Merry Christmas. They decorated their homes with colorful lights and a "Christmas tree" which could be any green tree available. Treats were prepared weeks in advance, particularly the special rum cake. It is said that pagan traditions show up in this winter holiday and in the harvest season in India. Such as decorating inside the house with greenery, giving thanks and exchanging gifts, visiting, and giving sweets to celebrate against the winter cold.

The spiritual aspect, although not on such a scale, is equally important to Christians and their neighbors. Midnight mass is significant for the Catholics, they often place small clay lamps burning with oil, on the roofs of homes to symbolize Jesus as the light of the world. Carols are sung by children's choirs going house to house. Fasting is done from the beginning of December to Christmas Day. In the Northeast, the snow is an added attraction.

The celebrations in India embrace a great deal of mirth and joy. The general excitement of Christmas is indeed a memorable experience.

CHRISTMAS—1950

George Francis Edward

$\mathcal{M}$any of my warm Christmas memories occurred in Grandpa Koss' apartment in New York City. It was a six-floor walkup built in 1910. My grandparents lived on the fifth floor, apartment seventeen. If you followed the toxic smell of mothballs, you couldn't miss it.

In those days, the entire block was a small, blue-collar neighborhood, and my grandparents knew the family history of each and every neighbor.

Pictured from left to right:
Tommy, Uncle, and George

Nowadays, you can buy an apartment in the same building for $800,000 or rent my grandparents' two-bedroom apartment for $3,400 per month. The block is no longer blue-collar, or even affordable to a middle-class family like my grandparents. Things certainly have changed!

In the above photo, taken in Grandpa's living room, my uncle Francis wears a cowboy outfit, complete with a six shooter. My brother Tommy also received a western pistol as a Christmas gift. As you can see, I did not receive a cowboy pistol. At the tender age of one, I was stuffing anything I could grab into my mouth. Shoes, rocks— everything went into my mouth. So, it probably was a good idea not to hand me a six shooter or a cap gun.

Grandpa and Uncle Francis would purchase a huge, noble fir tree, which occupied most of the tiny living room. Together they dragged the mammoth tree down the block and up five flights of stairs—no easy task. The top of the tree poked the ceiling in their apartment. The tree adornments were large and gaudy; for a little kid like me, their Christmas tree was a wonder to behold.

My Dad on the other hand, never wanted to spend more than ten dollars on a holiday tree. Noble firs were out of the question. He would visit the discount Christmas tree lots, and find the saddest, smallest, cheapest tree for sale. Even after selecting a god-awful tree, he would try to bargain down the price. If he got the sales price down to eight dollars, he was ready to buy.

Dad usually wound up with a skinny, picked-over tree, with large gaps in the middle of it. To fill those gaps, Dad scooped up half a dozen fir branches from the dirty, sawdusty ground. He took the tree home, drilled holes in the trunk, into which he inserted the orphan branches and secured them using white cotton string. He was trying to make an eight-dollar tree look like a twenty-five-dollar tree.

Of course, within a week, those fake branches turned brown, so our tree looked half brown and half green, with white cotton string draped in the middle. The first time I saw Charlie Brown's scraggly Christmas tree, I thought of our tree.

Our one Christmas toy was selected from the Sears & Roebuck catalogue. My parents would show us the catalogue and we selected the toy we wanted for Christmas. We might get socks or underwear along with our gift, but that one toy was the only gift we requested. Since my birthday fell on January 6th, I would check the Sears catalogue for my special Christmas toy as well as a possible birthday present, occurring just two weeks later.

Christmas in New York City was magical. Besides Grandpa's Christmas tree, the entire experience was beyond a little boy's dreams. If we arrived early enough, Grandpa would take us to the Central Park Zoo to see the silverback gorilla caged behind thick iron bars. Grandpa bought us a box of Cracker Jack at the zoo. I still remember munching the Cracker Jack and staring at the gorilla, who in turn stared at the Cracker Jack.

Back at Grandpa's house, Grandma was putting the finishing touches on our Christmas turkey dinner. Grandpa had a fabulous stuffing recipe. Once we sat down to dinner, my brother and I would eat quickly so we could resume playing with our Christmas toys. About this time, the arguing would start. Usually, Dad would pick on Mom because he thought she was drinking too much. Mom would defend herself and say she only drank "half a beer." Mom & Aunt Agnes liked to "share" beers; each drank half a can of Pabst Blue Ribbon. The problem was they didn't stop at one can. But Mom was never drunk, just happy and laughing. Everybody was happy. Except Dad.

My father was never happy. Even during Christmas. He seemed to be in a foul mood every day of the year. And Christmas was no different. It started when Dad parked the car. The parking situation in New York City pissed off my father. Dad could never find a parking space near Grandpa's apartment, and sometimes he had to park several blocks away. It seems that if somebody found a parking space in front of their apartment, they claimed it for months. It was an unwritten rule: you find a parking space and you leave your car in it for at least six months.

Thankfully, after playing with our toys, my brother and I fell asleep fairly early. My Mom would place us on Grandpa's bed, where we dozed off until everybody was ready to leave. As my brother and I slept in Grandpa's bed, I recall hearing the nonstop city street sounds: car horns, taxis, ambulances, barking dogs—a strange symphony of sounds for a small New Jersey boy.

Later, as my Dad drove home to the suburbs, screaming at my mother, analyzing in detail every one of her actions that he found objectionable, I looked out the back window and saw amazing sights. We would drive along flowery Park Avenue. The trees in the median were bedecked with Christmas lights. It was a dazzling sight, especially if you came from a backwater town in Jersey. The glowing lights whizzed by like meteors as we sped along the avenue.

As I gazed at the wondrous Christmas festival of lights; the beautiful green, red and yellow colored trees on Park Avenue—I could imagine myself flying through the stars. And if I focused intensely, I could block out the yelling in the front seat of the Chevy.

Ernest Hemingway once remarked, *'If you are lucky enough to have lived in Paris as a young man, then wherever you go for the rest of your life, it stays with you, for Paris is a moveable feast.'* For me, when I remember my childhood Christmas celebrations, I always come back to New York City, as a young boy, half asleep, peering out the back window of a speeding Chevy on Park Avenue, the lights glowing like meteors flying through a dark sky.

New York City is my "moveable feast" because no matter where I go, or how many years pass by, there dwells my "little boy's" joyful heart.

HAPPY MEMORIES

Elizabeth Jane Pryce

*A*lthough the picture of the nativity scene is not one from my collection, it brings back wonderfully happy memories, of a simpler life. When I was a child, still living in the West Indies with my grandparents, Christmas was a magical time. My grandmother, in particular, believed in a mixture of Christian beliefs, tradition and magic. She used them all, to make the best of any situation, especially Christmas. My grandfather's job was the tree, which was bought, found, or reinvented, as money allowed. One year it was a whitewashed old cherry tree! It looked incredible on Christmas morning! They may have sacrificed on the tree, but never on faith, tradition, or magic. All the decorations were hung on the tree, after I was in bed on Christmas Eve. For me it added to the special magic and excitement of Christmas.

My grandmother always made a Christmas Pudding and Cake, of which the pudding was the highlight of our Christmas dinner. Especially finding the tiny silver charms, she stirred into the pudding before it was cooked. They told our fortune for the following year! We would have a good laugh if my grandfather found a thimble or a bell!*

My grandmother always started the preparations for the pudding, the Sunday before Advent; a tradition apparently going back to medieval England. The pudding was supposed to be prepared with only thirteen ingredients, symbolizing Christ and the twelve apostles. Every family member took a turn stirring the mixture east to west, to honor the Magi! But as we were only three, she also invited neighbors. Although I was born in the middle of the twentieth century, my grandmother's traditions went back to a prior time. I found a copy of a recipe for an Old Testament Cake' in my aunt's cookbooks dated 1907. Now I wonder if that might have been the original source for her Christmas pudding and cake.

* The silver charms were a horseshoe for good luck, a button for a bachelor, a wishbone for granting a wish, a coin for good fortune, a thimble for a spinster and a bell for a bride.

Back in the colonial times, The Pudding, was seen as a symbol of unity throughout the British Empire. In 1927, the Empire Marketing Board, (EMB) manipulated the Royal recipe, to represent the Empire's many colonies. The final recipe included Australian currants, South African stoned raisins, Canadian apples, Jamaican rum, and English Beer, among other ingredients, all sourced from somewhere in the Empire. Brandy from Cyprus and nutmeg from the West Indies were also included. The final recipe, was sent to all the national newspapers and women's magazines. It was also printed and handed out to the public for free. Although by 1921, my great-grandmother had immigrated to America with her oldest daughter and three grandchildren and my Grandmother was already married and living with her husband and first baby in Australia, they most probably would have received magazines, newspapers and letters from the "Old Country."

The Nativity scene was different. It was put out slowly over the four weeks of Advent. On the first Sunday of December, our "stable," was placed on the cedar chest, that had been part of my grandmother's bridal trousseau. The stable was a small hemp-sack covered wooden box. Dry dirt and straw were sprinkled over the floor of the box, with small branches and leaves on the top. A large candle was placed in the crystal bowl, that was also part of the trousseau, and the story began!

On every Sunday, throughout lent, the miniature figures from the nativity scene were placed in the stable. The animal were placed first then Mary and Joseph, the Shepards, the Wise Men, and finally on Christmas Eve, the baby Jesus in the manger. We never went to church, but the symbolism and the real meaning of Christmas, were for my Grandmother, very important.

Presents were mostly homemade, or from families abroad, in England, Australia or America. They were always opened carefully. Packages were tied with ribbon or string, not sticky tape, making it easier to preserve the wrappings. These were used and reused, going back and forth between the countries, sometimes with stories attached; how long this paper had been in use, and who had it last, and even what was sent in it last time! All of which I loved. To this day, I hate tearing the wrapping from a present, because those traditions, are still wonderful memories.

Another tradition we always followed was having a lighted candle in the window to welcome a passing stranger in need. It was hinted that the stranger might be Christ or an Angel in disguise! It was the same for laying an extra place at the dinner table; being prepared to offer sustenance to a stranger in need. Again, this might be Christ or an Angel passing by! With today's social problems it is much harder; but I still put out artificial candles in the windows, and have an extra place serving ready. Just in case I get a surprise visit from someone out of town.

On the first Christmas after I was married, my grandmother gave me the nativity scene I had grown up seeing, every year for fourteen years. I was thrilled. I also inherited a few other decorations that had great memories for me; the tinseled angel, that sat at the top of the tree, the leaded tinsel that hung over the branches, a glow in the dark baby angel, and a few glass balls that were special to me. All were at least forty years old, when I started using them. They are almost ninety years old now!

The leaded tinsel and the angel of my childhood, have long since deteriorated and have gone, where all great memories go. The nativity collection and the glow in the dark baby angel are still with me, carefully unwrapped and rewrapped every year. The nativity pieces were made from plaster of Paris, by my second cousin, Ginger, when she was about ten! I bring them out every year, because I love to remember my grandmother, and how special she made Christmas.

The last part of our Christmas tradition each year, was to take down all the decorations on the twelfth day of Christmas, never a day earlier or later. The twelfth day in the Christian faith is the Feast of the Epiphany, the coming of the Magi.

For many years, while my own children were growing up, I kept up the tradition of putting up the tree and decorations on Christmas Eve, once they were in bed. I loved the way they still pretended that they believed in Santa and all the magic of Christmas, even when they were teenagers!

A CHRISTMAS TRADITION

Sandra J. S. Stanton

$\mathcal{A}$s I think back to my family's tradition of setting up a creche at Christmastime, I'm not sure when I learned the meaning of the creche—beyond a decoration. However, my family went to the Methodist Church, and I probably went to a kindergarten class, where a teacher would surely have read a story of the nativity to us. So, I would have been five when Mother, Daddy, my older brother David, and I began to decorate our house in Knoxville, Tennessee, in December 1943. Thus I would have looked at the little stable, made of David's Lincoln logs, and the figurines of Mary and Joseph, the babe in the manger, the shepherds and their sheep, and of course the angels, with some understanding of the story. We spread dried grass on floor of the stable and balanced a semicircle of cardboard covered with dark blue cellophane, on which stars had been pasted, against a stand behind the stable. I thought of it as sort of a Christmas dollhouse, but with a real and beautiful story, not like the stories I made up about the dollhouse Mother and Daddy had made for me to play with.

That simple, handmade creche remained a family tradition for as long as I lived with the family—in Knoxville, Chevy Chase, Idaho Falls, and then Manila. That is where, in 1955, I spent my last Christmas at home with my family, which had grown to include younger siblings Frank and Susie. A few months later, I returned to California to enter Scripps College, and David was already at the University of Chicago. I don't know what happened to the creche, as the diminished family moved on to Teheran, and then Monrovia, Liberia. Their belongings were in storage in various places, and we often lived half the world apart. My Christmases were spent with friends and relatives. I'm sure some of them had a creche, but I don't remember.

Not until I married Jim Stanton in 1959 was I home for Christmas again, in our little studio apartment in Glendale, California. I made a wreath for the door and we decorated a three-foot tree with lights, a few glass balls, and tinsel, but we had no creche. In 1962 we found a larger apartment before son Mike was born and then a little house after daughter Jill's birth. We had the usual decorations, with stockings of course, but no creche.

A few years later, Jim went to work for the CIA. Our first tour together was in Madrid, a magnificent city that put on a spectacular show for Christmas—with enormous firs decorated in white lights on most of the major boulevards. We lived in a house with high ceilings, so we brought home a ten-foot tree. We bought a lot of lights and ornaments, as well as a large star to put on the very top of the tree, which looked gorgeous in a windowed alcove of the living room. I wrote a poem about the light of the star bringing peace to the world, but we didn't have a creche.

Three years later, we moved to Monrovia, Liberia. There were no Christmas trees growing there! Many people decorated palms, and others (including us) ordered artificial trees from the Sears catalog. The branches were sparse, unable to hold even half the decorations we had brought with us from Spain. There were lots of parties, and Christmas was fun, but still we had no creche.

Two years passed. We returned to D.C. and moved into our house in Gaithersburg, Maryland, in early December 1974. Since we were going to Cape Cod for Christmas with all my siblings and their families, we didn't even put up a tree—just a wreath on the door and table decorations. The following year, we had a lovely six-foot tree, its branches heavily loaded with all the ornaments we had bought in Madrid. Of course, there were other Christmas decorations throughout the house, but we bought nothing new that year. Twenty years had passed since I had last seen the creche of my childhood.

A few months into 1976, we learned that we would be moving to Mexico City that summer. We arrived just before the Fourth of July, but it was September before we moved into an older but very comfortable house, not far from Chapultepec Park and just off the famed boulevard called the Reforma. The stucco walls and beamed ceilings, along with numerous mullioned windows and French doors, made it very inviting.

Not long after we moved in, we went to a ceramics workshop in search of lamps. We found a pair that were just perfect for our bedroom and promptly bought them. (They're still with us here in Bellingham!) Then, as we walked around the workshop, Jim and I saw a creche. Well, there were others, but only one drew us to it. The faces of Mary and Joseph, looking down at the babe that lay in a manger, were so sweet that you could almost see their love for the babe. Two angels looked on, and the three Kings were just arriving, bearing their gifts. A little drummer boy knelt near Mary, and three little lambs gathered around the manger.

They all came home with us that day, and we could hardly wait to arrange them on our mantle. We didn't think of making a stable or a backdrop of dark blue sky studded with stars. These little figures needed nothing more. And so has it been ever since that Christmas forty-three years ago, and will be again this year, when we unwrap them from the cotton wool in their own little box. What do they bring to us, these tiny figures of the nativity: the special spirit that fills our hearts as Christmas arrives once more, and perhaps a tear or two as we look back over so many Christmases past.

Short Stories

Stories written on a specific theme in 500 words or less.

HAIRCUTS

Sita C. Amba-Rao

*H*aircuts? What a topic for creative writing, what can I create out of this? Let me think. Maybe it's a good start: nothing, ground zero; here we go.

Over 60 year ago, when my kid sister was four years old. Lakshmi, my second mother, had made a promise to her favorite God, Venkateswara, Lord of Seven Hills in South India. If she gives birth to a healthy child, she would make the journey to the Seven Hills to give the gift of the first cut of the child's hair to him. This was a desperate act as she had had several miscarriages.

I did wonder at the time, did she think about whether the child might be a female, and about sacrificing her beautiful hair to Venkateswara. She did have a beautiful, healthy baby girl, Vimala, with a full head of hair. All promises were forgotten until the child approached the age of six. A promise to the god was not one lightly taken and the inevitable journey to the Seven Hills was due.

Lakshmi remembered arriving at the head clearing site. One could see little heads being shaved and ceremonial offerings being made by the open water tank. Some kids went through it happily, others reluctantly, with some fuss, and still others were awed and crying. This was their first experience, which they did not understand and they had to be consoled and cajoled.

"Oh, dear!" Lakshmi thought, "How can I put my child through this ordeal." She further agonized at the thought of her child's beautiful pigtails being cut off and her head shaved. She knew that the hair would grow back in a short while, but she could not accept the possibility, that bald could be beautiful as well. Fortunately, my father came up with a solution. "How about just giving a sample of the child's hair, no need for removing the whole harvest." He reminded her that the promise was for a "cut of the hair."

"This can range from a single strand to the entire head of hair, could it not?"

My mom, Lakshmi, was happy with her husband's idea. A few, random strands were cut, the promise fulfilled.

The God, Venkateswara, Lord of the Seven Hills, generously accepted what his devotee had offered. Lakshmi was grateful to the Lord. She saw her daughter grow up into a lovely young woman, who married and had a family of her own .

Vimala is now a grandmother of a lovely male toddler, and had recently arrived in America to spend time with him.

Moral of the story: never promise a bribe unless you know a way out.

HAIRCUTS

George Francis Edward

*H*aircuts are a sensitive subject for me. Always have been. In order to save money, my father insisted he cut his boys' hair. Up until I was a teenager, my father cut my hair.

My Dad was not a good barber. If he sheared sheep like he cut hair, all of his flock would have died.

The Bowl Look

Dad's solution to cutting hair was to place a bowl on your head, and to cut everything that wasn't covered by the bowl. When I went to school, kids would say to me "It looks like somebody put a bowl on your head!"

"I don't want to talk about it," was my usual reply.

Of course, Dad went to a barber for his own haircuts. He would never dream of having somebody mutilate his hair the same way he mutilated ours.

When I grew old enough to leave home, I grew my hair long. I sported long hair most of my adult life. I only started to get regular haircuts after reaching age forty.

At my declining age, I am constantly amazed at how women view a haircut.

When my wife, Dana, gets a haircut, she wants to talk about it as if it's a life-changing experience, and how she has been transformed into a new woman.

I tell her "I don't care, honey, it's just a haircut!" To me, the best haircut is the kind when you can't tell you got a haircut. If nobody notices, it was a good cut.

The Long-haired Look

I have been going to the same hair stylist for over ten years. She is a wonderful lady, originally from Vietnam.

I would refer to her as a barber, but I reserve that term for men. OK, call me sexist. I don't care. In my view, most barbers don't do perms or hair coloring, which my hair stylist offers.

I was amazed at the number of clients my stylist services. She is an independent contractor, in other words, she just rents the space at a hair salon.

I asked her how many clients it takes to make a hair-cutting business viable.

"Two hundred clients," she told me.

Wow! That's a large number. I notice many of her clients are middle-aged or older men like myself.

It takes my stylist about a half hour to cut my hair. Sometimes I will notice she has lined up her appointments like planes in an airport holding pattern. Each client comes into the salon every half hour on the nose. Like clockwork.

You know the best part? Nowhere in the salon will you find a plastic bowl that fits my head!

HAIRCUTS

Elizabeth Jane Pryce

I never liked getting my hair cut when I was young, the reason being, as Mummy described it, "I had rat's tails." I had hair that was neither curly nor straight, but hung in stringy strands around my face, if I didn't pull it up into a ponytail, with all the hair off my face. I never had a fringe; hair near my eyes always made me feel ill. Other than when the spiteful boys at school pulled my hair, it was relatively easy to manage.

If I wanted to go fancy for a change, I would have to endure Mummy putting my hair up in rags. She used strips of old cotton sheeting, torn into six-inch lengths and about half an inch wide. I would wash my hair and come and sit in front of her, she would then part and roll strands of hairs up in the rags and tie them tight. That's the part that hurt. Small hairs would get caught up in the rags and pull terribly. Mummy would glibly quote with a cheerful smile, "There is no pleasure without pain." Once the rags were out, I would enjoy lovely curly hair for the day!

When I was about the age of sixteen or seventeen, I was finally persuaded to have my long hair cut. At first it looked nice, a bob with the ends curling under at chin level. Annoying problems began to appear not long afterward, though. Some of the curled under hair would flip up; half would be curled up and other half curled under! It took a lot of pain and anguish from rollers at night and frustration and time to get it right in the morning. Then, the cut ends of the hair starting causing a nasty red rash along my chin line. As a teenager who had never had a skin problem, this was a problem! Since I couldn't put the hair back on, I decided that maybe if I had it cut shorter, the problems of both curls and rashes would go away.

I made another appointment with the local hairdresser. That was when my hair became a major disaster. The finished cut looked like my little sister had attacked my hair in the night! It was certainly short now! It was unevenly cut, all over my head. I was very embarrassed. But the saddest part, was seeing the horrified look on the face of a boy I liked and had hoped would ask me out. He had finally noticed me after the first haircut!

TO CUT OR NOT TO CUT

Sandra J. S. Stanton

I must admit that I don't remember this story myself, but my mother related it to me when she gave me a braided lock of my hair. When she later gave me a carved wooden trunk from Taiwan, I tucked it away with many other bits of memorabilia that reside in the trunk, which is a splendid place to look for family history and other story ideas; and its contents continue to grow.

As a youngster, I had light brown hair of a texture that tangled easily. It was kept short until I was about four. Then I begged to let it grow and wear it in curls, which my mother and grandmother produced by rolling it up with strips of cloth—from old sheets, I believe. I loved the curls, but not the tangles that had to be painfully brushed or combed out. So, I agreed to wear it in braids, except on special occasions, but braiding was not yet something I could do for myself.

In 1944, I turned six and was very excited about entering first grade. I got to ride the big yellow school bus. But our house was the third stop, and I had to be ready to climb aboard at 7:45. That was when I was used to getting up! Mother helped me start learning to get up earlier, and we made a chart of what I needed to do. The last thing before breakfast was to braid my hair. Uh-oh. I could sort of do it, but I was slow. The chart broke down, and so did I, when I reached "Braid hair." And with all the commotion, my two-year-old brother Frank often woke up and let the world know that he wanted his breakfast—Now!

Mother told me, "I have to get up, get dressed, and make breakfast [which always included juice, eggs, toast, and cereal] early for all of us, now including Frank. I simply have no time to braid your hair. You'll have to manage to do it yourself or go to school with your hair flying into a tangle. Or… you can simply get a haircut."

"No!" I cried. "Then I couldn't have long curls on special occasions either!" [Oh, the vanity of a six-year-old!]

She realized, then, that losing my long hair was a major thing. So she said, "What if we go downtown this Saturday, get your hair cut at the beauty parlor, and then have lunch and go shopping?"

'Hmm,' I thought, 'the haircut's gonna happen. And I've never been to a beauty parlor, or out to lunch and shopping, like ladies!' "Okay," I said, and we did!

FALL COLORS IN INDIANA:
Zionsville and Brown County State Park

Sita C. Amba Rao

$\mathcal{Z}$ionsville, Indiana is a quaint little town listed on the internet as one of the desirable small towns across America. In contrast, to the well-known flat lands of mid-America, Zionsville has a hilly landscape, which turns into a carpet of orange, red and yellow shades in fall. "Easy going vibe and community spirit radiate around brick streets, where independent retailers elbow up against locally owned eateries."*

Brown County State Park is something else! It is located in South Central Indiana, close to the Tennessee/Kentucky border, near Indiana University-Bloomington and an hour away from Indianapolis. The Park has a large array of colors in fall and is called the "Little Smokies." after the Smokey Mountains. With 1.3 million visitors a year, it is famous for its scenic views of hills. It has a large variety of trees, which transformed the entire Park in the autumn. The best time to see the transformation is from late September to early November. The elevated vistas in the Park, provide panoramic views of the trees and their vast array of colors.

Have you ever wondered why leaves change color in the fall? The leaves have different chemicals that determine the pigment and color in them. Chlorophyll is the dominant chemical. Because of cooler nights and shorter periods of sunlight, Chlorophyll reduces, and other colors gradually surface. The different chemicals in the leaves produce different hues, such as: Tannins for brown or tan, Anthocyanins for deep red and purple and Carotenoids for yellow and orange.

Similarly, certain trees have specific colored leaves: Oaks, brown; Hickory, golden bronze; Dogwood, purple-red; Birch, bright yellow; Poplar, golden yellow; Sassafras, orange; and Tupelo, red. Maples produce a wide range of colors; orange-red, yellow,

* Zionsville at Google

scarlet and green. Some trees change colors earlier than others. The Tulip tree is first, Sycamores and Walnuts next, but they don't have much color change. Oaks and Beech are the last to change and sometimes retain their leaves throughout the winter.

How about Washington State's fall colors? While leaves turn into lovely yellows, the contrasting shades are not as vivid as in the eastern states. Picture Lake, on the way to Mt. Baker's Artist Point, is as its name suggests, a picture perfect view of water and colorful trees in the fall. Their reflections, crystal clear in the lake.

Another view I like is Barkley Boulevard and the tree lining Barkley Hill, where I lived!

Nature is wonderland!!

JOSEPH MALLORD WILLIAM TURNER

George Francis Edward

*O*ne of J.M.W. Turner's favorite colors was chrome yellow. Turner was known as the "Painter of Light." Unfortunately, chrome yellow turns brown when exposed to light.

Turner was widely criticized for being more concerned about the fresh look of his paintings than their devastating propensity to fade or turn brown.

When Turner's friend, William Winsor, cautioned Turner about using pigments that will fade, Turner remarked, "Your business Winsor, is to make colour. Mine is to use them."

Since Turner utilized colors to delineate the borders of objects, once the color faded, you were left with an amorphous blob. It is hard to distinguish any shapes at all.

Turner used carmine pigments in his paintings, despite being told the pigments would fade. It is said that Turner wiped tobacco juice and stale beer on his paintings for effect. He even spit on the paintings. All these effects were intended to enhance the bright colors.

I recall viewing Turner's paintings at the Tate Gallery in London. The experience was unsettling. On the one hand, you could see the spectacular chrome yellow and reds that he used for great effect. But on the other hand, you noticed how dry, brown and faded the paintings had become. You knew these were once magnificent works of art, but what was left was anything but magnificent.

What artist would not want to preserve his art for posterity? What painter wouldn't care if the quality of his pigments declined during his lifetime?

If you view some of Turner's yellow paintings, like Sunrise with Sea Monsters, or The Slave Ship, how much better these paintings would be if the pigments looked fresh, and not faded.

Turner was known for the fantastic imagery in his paintings. Perhaps, the fact that his paintings over time coalesced into indistinct colors has added to this imagery. If you cannot clearly define the subjects in Turner's paintings, then interpretation and speculation are endless.

Other great artists used pigments that faded. Van Gogh's "The Bedroom" contains faded red pigments.

"Paintings fade like flowers," Van Gogh once wrote his brother Theo. "All the more reason to boldly use them too raw; time will only soften them too much."

This brings us back to our main argument. Was it better to use bright colors and pigments to create a masterpiece, even though those same pigments would not survive the painter's lifetime?

If we follow the lives of Turner and Van Gogh, the answer is yes. Their colors were bold and daring. Their motto was 'carpe diem' —seize the day, make the most of the present time, and give little thought to the future.

MY FAVORITE COLOR AND OTHER THINGS

Elizabeth Jane Pryce

$\mathcal{B}$lue was my favorite color for a long time. It was a cool yet vibrant color in the heat of the tropical sun. Even today, I have a pale blue ceiling, on which the refracted morning light from crystals in the window, create colorful rainbows, across my bed.

Blue is the color of the sky today, pale where it meets the horizon. White clouds high above the islands look like the snow on the Olympic Mountains, which I could see if I had telescopic vision.

Later, on the beach, the sun is warm on my cheek, the cold northeast wind has subsided. The Pacific Willow trees along the embankment shine with a faint orange glow in the sunlight. Later in the month, the orange will become darker and in another month the buds will become long thin pale green leaves. I stop and sit for a few minutes, throwing small pebbles for my dog. People always seem happy on the beach, even when it is cold.

The water is steely blue and I suspect, very cold, yet some dogs are happily running in after sticks. They come out wagging their tails, all ready to go again. We met and greeted many dogs on the way down the beach, including an eight week old toy Australian Shepherd puppy. She is afraid of Henry, and yikes at him. He must seem like a giant to her three pounds against his nineteen. Fully grown she will only weigh approximately twelve pounds!

As Henry, Daisy and I leave the beach and head up Seaview Ave, the winds barrels down the steep road hitting us with a blast of wintry air. Halfway up, I get a call saying we have lost power in the neighborhood. I am not looking forward to a chilly evening and no dinner. Then I remembered, the last time the power went out, I had found my old camping gas stove stored in the attic. I will, at least be able to make a cup of tea. Dinner could wait, as I breakfasted at midday today!

It has been a good day, one of many achievements. I talked to my sister for a long time this morning, as well as my mother and my niece, all of whom live in England. My niece was feeding her six-month-old baby, whipped porridge with fresh raspberries. Baby Evie, weighing in at less that five pounds at birth, was doing extremely well, kicking her legs and smiling with every mouthful! I had also finished the ten little dresses I had been making for the children at Cameron's Orphanage in Zambia; my brother and his fiancé's charity. I was excited because the first three were very difficult. I felt like the completion, took years off my life.

THE COLOR WHITE

Sandra J. S. Stanton

*T*here is no question about it. In the contemporary world, white is a color—not the absence of color. It is defined by many hues, or shades—for instance, winter white, bone white, ivory white, snow white, warm and cool white. But the best way to imagine the color white is in its context. Let's see!

I remember learning to swim in the Gulf of Mexico, running across the sparkling white sand of a Florida beach toward the aqua blue water, where my Aunt May awaited me. The sand was so bright it hurt my eyes. It was as white as the salt in the shaker on the kitchen table. Only five at the time, I had to taste it to find out. No, It was not salt.

After my swimming lesson, we lay on the sand, looking up at the fluffy white clouds, but white clouds are always gently shaded by blues and grays. Otherwise, we wouldn't be able to see animals, or faces, or the other fascinating objects we can see in the clouds.

The first snow I saw, in Tennessee, rivaled Florida's white sand in color and was even more exciting. All bundled up, I went out to play in the snow, but the first thing I did was put a handful in my mouth. It tasted cold, icy cold. After dinner, my mother made a surprise dessert. Bringing in a pot of fresh white snow from a drift outside the back door, she spooned it into bowls, sprinkled sugar over the snow, and topped it with cream. It was so good! Years later, I made snow ice cream for our children in Virginia, digging fresh snow out of the four-foot drifts of that 1965 winter's blizzard!

For me, white was a happy color, until my brother David suffered an abdominal hemorrhage and spent two weeks in the hospital. When I visited him, the pale color of his face and the white color of the walls, the curtains, the sheets, and the nurses' dresses evoked only sadness, until he got well!

Years passed, as they do. Jim and I were to be married, in California. My parents and younger siblings were living abroad, and the wedding preparations were up to us, mostly me. First things first—my dress. I found just the right pattern, then a pure white flower-embossed fabric, and finally some delicate white lace to insert at the neck and in bands on the skirt, as well as to make a short-veiled white headband. It took three weeks to make, but my wedding outfit was just perfect. I have it still.

MAIL

Sita C. Amba Rao

*W*ho was it who sang, *"Hey mail man."*

In the past, In India, one could never visualize a female, mail carrier. Only men could apply for the job. But some women, were smart and bold. They took advantage of the equal opportunity law, and saw their chance. They took to the roads as postal employees, delivering mail. Their uniforms were saris with fitting blouses, which they wore even in the hot sun.

It wasn't long before courier companies, such as Fed Ex and other Indian entrepreneurs began delivering packages to people's homes. The delivery business was booming, catering to official transactions, as well as consumer business. With current behemoth online businesses such as Amazon.com, there were added opportunities for women, especially if they spoke English, or better still had a college education. A common language is needed in a country of diverse languages.

The smart women started with saris. But as times changed, they changed. The *Punjabi dress*, or Salwar and Kurthas, became popular all over India. Salwars are loose fitting pants and Kurthas are long tops with side slits. This style evolved to well-fitting pants and Kurthis, which is a shorter version of the Kurthas, with smaller side slits. If you look around you will see them worn by many Americans.

The necks are styled in different ways, like the tee-shirts—Henley or V-neck. Being elegant, yet practical, these have also been adopted in America, although not under the same name. The men wore khaki uniforms of various styles, depending on the hiring company.

Dress aside, the couriers, both men and women go around in two-wheeler scooters or motorcycles. They wear helmets, as required by law. Do not forget the ubiquitous water bottle and the cell—ah, mobile—phone. These couriers go about the delivery of packages or mail, get a signature, have a drink of water, and off they go. If you give a tip or a snack, they don't say, "No," unless there is a company policy against tipping, assuming they are well paid.

What about the snail mail, one might ask. In contemporary times, with the ever present mobile phones and texting, very few people want the inconvenience and inefficiency of a traditional mail business. The courier-using population is hedonistic. They are the *Can't wait*, and *Want it now*, people. The large middle class population. As a result, the Indian government's postal service has to be in sleep mode, until an occasional someone clicks, then the service wakes up and goes into action! Unless, there is some kind of public-private collaboration, as in America, capitalism will continue to thrive, for better or worse.

MAIL

George Francis Edward

A tenant at my condominium complex accused me of scraping his brand new Porsche. Actually, he said I backed up into it, crushing the left front fender. His Porsche was white, and he said he knew I hit his car because there were red paint marks on it, and my Volkswagen beetle was the only red car parked nearby.

"What?" I replied. "I never hit your car!"

"Yes—you did!" he insisted.

This fellow was a rich foreign exchange student, studying here on an Iranian visa. I couldn't pronounce his name because it had a bunch of h's and k's in it. All I knew was that he was absolutely wrong, yet for some reason, was determined to make me pay for an accident that had nothing to do with me.

"You always park your car in the Emergency Fire Vehicle zone," I told him. The reason that area was marked with red stripes was to warn people not to park there. I guessed what probably happened, was that somebody drove along the edge of the parking lot in the darkness and gashed this guy's Porsche. Besides being illegally parked, I suspected his Porsche was jutting out into the street, so anybody could have clipped it as they drove by.

"Your car is red and there was red paint on my front fender," he said.

"So what does that mean?" I asked. "You have no witnesses."

"Yes, I saw you do it."

"Really? When? I leave for work at 6:30 am, and it is dark outside when I leave my condo."

"I happened to be jogging by and I saw you hit my car."

This guy was making false accusations against me, adding blatant untruths, and perjuring himself to back it up.

"I'm going to call the police and report you," he said.

"Good! Do it!" I shouted.

The next day I got a call from a San Diego police officer. I explained my side of the story. I mentioned that he was charging me with hit and run, but the tenant had no witnesses (besides himself) and no evidence. The officer said she wasn't going to follow up on her report because she suspected he fabricated the entire story.

About one hundred mailboxes are clustered in the front of our condo building so the mailman can deliver all of our mail with just one stop. Next to the cluster mailbox is a bin, where you can place any mail mis-delivered to your box.

I noticed the foreign student had received his California Driver's License. I grabbed it from the bin and chucked it down the trash chute. Smiling, I walked away. Karma.

MAIL

Elizabeth Jane Pryce

*A*s a child, on the island of St. Vincent, receiving mail was always fun. It meant a trip into town once a week and a visit to the post office, where Mummy and I would stand in the queue until we reached the grill and the post office lady. She would run down the line of open boxes behind her and pull out the mail with our name on it. Around the Christmas holidays, there could be a box waiting for us. Daddy would have to come with the car to pick it up. Sometimes the boxes would go directly to Corea's General Store, owned by my Aunty Gussie and where Daddy worked.

Because of the political unrest at the time, I found that things had changed a bit, when I went back in 1969. The island was fighting for independence, from the United Kingdom, and being "White Colonials," as we were often referred to, some situations could be dangerous. Now, going with my aging grandmother, (Mummy), to the post office helped to offset any jousting and heckling, that she might be subjected to.

Not long before I left St Vincent in 1964, regional post offices were built. We had one at the end of our road. Back then I would walk the mile of so down the road with my dog Bingo and pick up the mail. It was by watching this lady, in the post office, that I finally learnt to knit! Often I would continue on the main road towards town and turn off on the next road, above the river. This would take me to the mental asylum and the foot path, that went down along the high brick wall of the asylum and across the river. I would almost be back at our property edge.

For a while, until my known world fell out beneath me, it was fun writing long letters back home to Mummy and Daddy and my friends, telling them about the differences in schools and the wonderful and exciting things I would be doing at the weekends. All that changed after only a few months. I was told Mummy and Daddy were actually my grandparents and my mother was their youngest daughter. But I was forbidden to tell anyone that I knew! With my naive, concrete child's logic, how could I write to them with a secure mind, happy to tell them what I was doing.

It was a difficult time for me and letters ceased for a few years. In those years I forced myself to become more fully integrated into my school. I did made friends, and even met my first husband. After he asked me to marry him, I asked my fiancé to write to *Daddy* asking for my hand in marriage. I knew he would be very happy to receive that kind of letter. My grandparents came to England permanently two years later in 1972, in time to be at our wedding.

MAIL OF A DIFFERENT MILLENNIUM

Sandra J. S. Stanton

"*M*argaret!" yelled Richard, "Where is Robin? That squire is never around when I want him."

"Oh, Richard, whatever is the matter? Did Lord Andrew scold you for being late to Mass this morning?"

"No, no, no," and I wasn't late to Mass. But M'lord told us that Lord William is holding a tournament next month, and he is expecting a perfect performance from our knights. We must practice jousting every day, and you may be sure that M'Lord will be watching. The problem is that my mail is in disrepair. Many broken chain links need replacing, and the entire suit must be cleaned and polished. That is Robin's job, you know, and all my armour must be ready for the first practice day after tomorrow. He's probably hiding somewhere.

"Oh yes, I need a new tunic. Can Elizabeth sew well enough to make one? If not, we'll have to find a more experienced seamstress, who can also reline my helmet. The padding has worn thin. But the main thing is the mail. It must be gleaming, or M'lord will certainly scold me."

"Calm down, Richard. I'll find Robin and start him to work immediately. Elizabeth can handle the sewing, and I myself will embroider Lord Andrew's coat of arms on your tunic. We'll get a maid to scrub the mail with sand and vinegar, and Robin can do the polishing. He must also see that your steeds are well groomed."

"Oh, Margaret, my darling wife, I thank thee," said Richard, as he gave her a kiss. "I must be off. Lord Geoffrey is meeting with all our knights to share the knowledge of siege warfare that he gained in battle against the Turks. There may be another crusade, you know."

Margaret shuddered at the thought, but she put on a brave face and gave Richard a weak smile. She would make sure that Robin shined her dear knight's chainmail until it gleamed, and his helmet until she could see her face in it. Then she looked in her trunk and selected her newest gown to wear to supper that evening—the royal blue with the gold bodice. There would be music and dancing after supper! In addition to jousting practice, the knights had been practicing new dance steps; so had their ladies, of course.

While Richard was learning all about siege warfare, she would go to the chapel and pray hard that there would be no more crusades—at least for awhile. She hadn't yet said anything to her amorous and handsome husband, but all the signs were evident. Their first child would be born in a few months.

RAIN, IT'S A PAIN

Sita C. Amba Rao

*R*ain can be a blessing, but also a pain! Earlier this week, I remember, the dark, gloomy, cloudy day, damp and drizzly all around? I was alone at home, late in the afternoon. Our neighbor, Ben said that they were moving down to California, his wife, who was from there could not bear the gloom anymore. Ben was a lifelong Seattleite and he loved this weather, but he was willing to move. Darn, anything for love! I wondered if this was part of a prenuptial contract, to move, if she couldn't put up with our Pacific northwest weather!

As for me, I decided to get over my blues, and change my attitude towards the rain, the Bellingham rain was not going to change. If the mountain will not go to Muhammad, then Muhammad should go to the mountain!

So, I sat, closed my eyes, and transported myself to the rainy seasons of India. My first image was the best. It was the Kerala State in the Southwest corner of India. The city, Trivandrum, where we domiciled for four years, was by the Arabian Sea. The clouds gathered and rain poured, until it seemed to wash the sky clear. Umbrellas, which had popped open in the wind and rain, some of them blowing inside out, were closed or put away. Because, lo and behold, the sun was out to say, "Hello," spreading its sunshine over the entire city. Rainbow to boot! What a treat! Monsoons came to Kerala in May.

Then, there was Andhra State. Rains would start in July, sometimes with heavy downpours. This was a gift to the farmers, who at other times may have suffered from drought, devastating their crops. When this happened, the farmers would hold desperate prayers to Indra, the Hindu Vedic deity of rain.

Finally, there was Mumbai, with heavy monsoon rains in July and August. Did anyone bother? It never seemed to be a problem. Commuters rushed to catch suburban trains to get to their jobs in the metro area, others scurried about to get their chores done. The ubiquitous, colorful umbrellas were always handy with whatever rain gear one could afford. It ranged from *Stoppers Shop*; the sleek westernized department store, to sidewalk vendors, hawking their goods and haggling over prices, but never losing a good profit!

Ah! Back to reality. All this fantasizing, led me to look on the bright side of the dark day. As a friend wrote in her e-mail the other day, "I am actually enjoying the rain. I love the sun, but it sure makes it easier to work, when it's cloudy out,"

Inspired, I went out and let the rain drops fall on my head!

RAIN

George Francis Edward

$\mathcal{M}$y wife and I spent over two decades in San Diego. When it rained there, it was a national emergency. Traffic snarled, people were suddenly wet, and nobody knew what to do! Oh, the horror!

"Alas! Alas!" San Diego locals wailed like bushmen, "moisture is falling from the sky! The Gods are angry!" All of a sudden, San Diego meteorologists were hard pressed to explain the phenomenon. They used terms like "half an inch" to explain a downpour. Of course, where we come from, we use the term "feet" to describe a heavy downpour.

In the great Pacific Northwest, it makes news when it DOESN'T rain, not when it does.

However, I have discovered many things I dread from this wet climate, other than rain.

Because we live in a rain forest, everything around us is green. By "green" I mean covered in moss. Moss covers your car, your house, your driveway—indeed, green moss covers everything. Every few years, I hire a power washer company to blast the moss off our roof. If we did not do this, the moss would grow into the composite shingles and destroy them; pretty soon, plants and trees would be growing out of our attic!

Rain forest living means brush and weeds thrive in the spring and summer. I purchased a grass hog, a hedgehog, a pruning saw, a lopper and God knows what else to beat back the encroaching brush. You feel like the flora has a mind of its own and is intent on strangling you to death in your sleep.

Constant rain means everything is wet most of the time. I am amazed at how many people in the Pacific Northwest wear open toed shoes. "Socks and sandals" look stupid to me, but in certain areas of Bellingham, and in the entire city of Portland, it is standard footwear. I guess I like my toes to be warm and dry, not cold and wet. But that's just me.

Finally, because of the climate, I am forced to change the windshield wipers on my automobile every few years. The rubber hardens, and the wipers begin to fail. Strange, but in San Diego, I never used my windshield wipers. Because it rarely rained in San Diego, I actually forgot how to operate the damn things. When it did rain (maybe once or twice during the winter), I would frantically turn my left and right blinker on, trying to figure out which friggin' lever controlled the wipers. It would take a few minutes to relearn how to operate the wipers, because I hadn't turned them on in six months or so!

True story.

RAIN

Elizabeth Jane Pryce

*W*hen I lived in the tropics as a child, rain always seemed to be a special event. The rainy season was typically from June to December, with hurricanes sometimes happening around August and September. When the weather was hot and humid, a tar-fragrant steam would rise off the roads when it rained. One time as I was racing home to help prepare for the coming hurricane, I found myself in a ditch after a rather sharp bend in the road! Once home, I helped Daddy hammer the loose nails into our tin roof and put the wooden shutters on the windows.

It was this hurricane that ripped out and destroyed the agricultural community of Tobago, just off the coast of Venezuela, but it was also one of the best time of my young life. After the storm had passed, I played with Daddy, making and sailing paper boat down our watery road! To me it was a raging river, and I was the captain of many boats.

Before the start of the rainy season, Daddy would try to dig enough ditches running through the middle of his passion fruit arbors. He was hoping to catch and hold the rainfall. I would dam up a small section of the river so I could catch fish. Usually I only caught crawfish or very tiny fish, which I had to throw back. One time, I caught a large enough crawfish to cook and eat, which I did in a sawn off tin over a bush fire.

Some ordinary rainy days could be boring and in my out of tune voice, I would sing the nursery rhyme, "Rain, rain go away, come again another day"—but add my own version for the last line, "I want to go out to play." Sometimes Daddy, who would be sitting in his chair fiddling with the radio tuner knob, would chime in and say, "Daddy wants to play!" And Mummy, who might be either in the kitchen making bread or preparing feed for the chickens, or at her typewriter writing a letter, would chime in as well, but she would say, "Mummy doesn't want to play!" At this point it could get really ridiculous, and we might all join in singing, "Hands, knees and

Boomps-a-Daisy," until Mummy would flick her teacloth at us and say, "That's enough hilarity for today!"

I loved being in the sea, but of all the peculiar childish behavioral traits; I didn't like swimming in the sea while it was raining! I would run out of the water, saying, "I am getting wet!" "You are already wet," Daddy would reply. But it didn't matter, I wouldn't go back into the sea until the rain was over. My other intense dislike was oozy mud, which of course happened quite often in the rainy season!

RAINING NOTES IN SHARPS AND FLATS

Sandra J. S. Stanton

A little reminiscence about rain in songs: from Broadway musicals to movies, and even those little round black discs we called 'records.'

Let's start way back—to Al Jolson singing "April Showers" in a 1921 Broadway hit called "Bombo." You remember it: "Though April showers may come your way, they bring the flowers that bloom in May. So, if it's raining, have no regrets, because it isn't raining rain, you know...it's raining violets."

Then there was an early 1930s movie titled "Melody for Two," which I confess I never saw, but I do know that it bequeathed us a hauntingly melancholy love song that begins with "The leaves of brown came tumbling down, remember—in 'September in the Rain.'" The song ends just as sadly with "Though spring is here, to me it's still September—that 'September in the Rain.'" Guy Lombardo kept this song's popularity alive for decades.

Who could ever forget the title song of the 1952 musical film, "Singing in the Rain"? Although the song, and its story, made it to Broadway in 1983, most people remember the movie and its stars, Debbie Reynolds, Donald O'Connor, and Gene Kelly—especially Kelly, head over heels in love, swinging around a lamppost as he dances and sings the famous lyrics, "I'm singing in the rain, just singing in the rain. What a glorious feeling, I'm happy again..."

A favorite of many, I'm sure, is "'Raindrops Keep Falling on My Head,' but that doesn't mean my eyes will soon be turning red—Crying's not for me, 'cause I'm never gonna stop the rain by complaining, because I'm free, nothing's worrying me." Well, not then, in Wyoming, but there comes a gunfight, in a place far away, in the 1969 movie, "Butch Cassidy and the Sundance Kid," for which this song was written by Hal David and Burt Bacharach.

We'll end in Edwardian England. In a 1956 Broadway hit, a Cockney flower girl, named Eliza Doolittle, is plying her wares in London's Covent Garden when she is approached by Colonel Pickering and Professor Henry Higgins, a phoneticist. Laughing at Eliza's atrocious accent, Pickering challenges Higgins to convert the girl's speech into that of a lady. Eliza agrees to accompany them to Higgins' home, where her schooling begins. Little progress is made until one evening, all of them exhausted, Higgins puts a recording on the gramophone—"The Rain in Spain Falls Mainly on the Plain." Then suddenly, as if someone had turned on a switch, these words flow from Eliza's mouth in the most ladylike accent. The men proclaim her to be "My Fair Lady," who never would have come into being if a little rain hadn't fallen on the plain in Spain.

TULIPS AND MOXIE, MY LOVE

Sita C.Amba-Rao

$\mathcal{T}$his story is addressed to my love, my husband, Chinna, or Kanna, my two nicknames for him.

My trip to tulip town; La Conner, was special for me. Prasada Rao and Chandrabala visited last weekend and instead of going to Vancouver, destiny took us to the tulip fields.

I pour out my sentiment to you, my love, as I cherish that trip. The weather was lovely, and the fields were in full bloom, in a full spectrum of color. This time, every step I took inside the Tulip House, the showroom and out in the field, memories of our walking together came back to me. Every bloom was precious and I felt you there with me.

In the field, we rode on the trolley. As it meandered around the fields, I had the time and space to take in each row of blooms with pleasure, as you would eat every bite of your cheese cake with lust! Dear Kanna, there were so many varieties, I learned about just a few of them. Here are a few interesting ones:

Purple: Victoria's Secret and Purple dream.

Black: Black Hero, Queen of the night.

Ballerina: Orange and marigold with sweet scent, petals arching away, in dance.

Line Dance: Double tulip with red drops on white petals.

Monte Carlo: Sulphur yellow with amazing smell.

Above all, what caught my eye was the Flaming Parrot, the red and yellow tulip, which you liked. I brought home a bouquet for you. Also Chinna, I brought a single floating flower for my writing friends, where we were sharing tulip stories.

So here I am with a chance for relieving my burden of culpability, for your unfulfilled desire to plant tulip bulbs in our yard. Now when I look at tulips I cherish our memory, thus trying to ease my guilt of not being able to fulfill that one simple wish of yours. I imagine you saying, *"Be real, I know how you cringe at having to dig into the soil, plant and care for plants, despite your love of flowers. Besides, you have no green thumb. Remember, the bulbs you brought one time, how they withered away for lack of attention?"* Well, what can I say, but I am moved by your understanding.

As always—well mostly—you are the rational Moxie for me. In the same vein, allow me; as long as there are gardeners, masters or not, like Jane and writers of tulips Sandra, Joan and George, and all of us sharing our written stories, you can listen in and enjoy!

TULIPS

George Francis Edward

*I*n 2005 I planted tulips around our driveway. This was the first time I had planted tulips, so I wasn't sure what I was doing. The flowers popped up and showed their colors. However, the next year less than half the bulbs bloomed. I then discovered tulips need unearthing at season's end and replanting in the fall. Frankly, this was too much effort for me, owing to the hard ground I tilled near the driveway. Therefore, I abandoned tulips as possible flowers in our yard.

Tulips

Our yard is overrun by deer. We live next to a forest, so the deer were here first. I've grown to tolerate deer; I just need to adjust for their damage. Besides eating anything that looks beautiful to humans (like most flowers), deer munch on ground cover (ivy), and the larger bucks destroy the young trees in the yard by scent marking. The bucks rub their foreheads and antlers against the bark, ripping it off the tree. At least half a dozen trees in our yard show signs of deer rub. The large bucks leave scat along their trail—piles of bullet-shaped pellets.

I tried planting tulips in other places in the yard, where the ground is soft and full of black topsoil. But those places are where deer roam, so the tulips were devoured as soon as they bloomed. After much experimentation, I discovered a few flowers that the deer seem to shun—daffodils and Pacific coast irises. Sadly, daffodils require replanting in the fall, so I

Pacific Iris

eliminated them for the same reason as the tulips, which leaves me with the irises.

My sister, Lorraine, told me how to prevent the deer from attacking our trees. She said to hang a bar of Lifebuoy soap on the tree, and the scent will discourage the deer. I did as my sister suggested. I attached a bar of Lifebuoy soap to a string and hung it from one of our trees.

The next day I found the Lifebuoy soap on the ground. It had been chewed in half by a hungry deer. I expect the deer grew bored munching on the ivy and tulips in the yard, so they decided to try an "after dinner mint," namely the scented Lifebuoy soap. At any rate, I told my sister her deer remedy might work for East Coast deer, but our West Coast species are voracious!

Spring Plum Blossom *

On a final note, I planted a few flowering trees, which seem to beautify the yard, and the flowers are high enough on the trees so the deer can't reach them. Here is one such lovely flower: a spring plum blossom.

* Original color photograph appears in the Whatcom Educational Credit Union calendar for March 2020.

TULIPS

Elizabeth Jane Pryce

$\mathcal{T}$ulips are the harbinger of spring. Their bright colors liven up the bare soil of the passing winter. I have spent many enjoyable days, wandering as a family through the brightly colored fields of Mount Vernon and La Connor, in Washington. It was at the Roozengaarde in Skagit Valley that I ordered my first $100 worth of bulbs! Most of them have long since disappeared, but one still comes up every year. It has always been my favorite; a variety called Miranda, which I originally planted in my garden over twenty years ago. It is a vibrant red peony-like tulip. In full sunshine, it can measure up to four inches across, when fully open.

But what fascinates me the most, is the history behind these extraordinary bulbs. Originally cultivated in the Ottoman Empire, it was imported into Holland in the sixteenth century. In 1593, when Carolus Clusius, a botanist from Vienna, was invited to supervised the creation of a botanical garden at Leiden University, he also brought his prized tulips with him. Amongst many other new and exotic plants, he planted a tulip garden. The following spring his bulbs bloomed, and a craze was started!

By the early seventeenth century, the desire to own a tulip bulb reached extraordinary high levels and *Tulip mania* was born. As the craze grew, bulbs became so expensive, that people were known to exchange entire properties in order to own a single bulb! During the tulip mania, an infection of the bulbs called the "breaking virus," created incredible variations of delicately feathered patterns in the flowers. This patterning was so highly valued, that growers went to extraordinary lengths to produce these effects. Unfortunately, the virus also weakened the bulb, reducing the number of offsets produced. But these remarkable patterns were so highly prized, that the prices soared and the market eventually crashed. Today the virus is mostly eradicated. The variegated and feathered varieties we have now, are a result of breeding and are part of a group known as the Rembrandts; so named because Rembrandt painted some of the most admired tulips of his time.

In the Ottoman Empire, the tulip was seen as a holy symbol. The word is originally thought to come from the Persian language, since when written in Arabic, it has the same letters as the word for Allah. According to Iranian folklore, a red tulip grows where a martyr has fallen. In Christianity, the white tulip represents forgiveness and the purple represents royalty. Calvinism used the acronym T.U.L.I.P* for the five points of their faith!

---

* Calvinism has five essential tenets T.U.L.I.P which stands for Total depravity, Unconditional election, Limited atonement, Irresistible grace, and Perseverance of the saints.

TIPTOEING THROUGH THE TULIPS

Sandra J. S. Stanton

*D*o you remember that old song, "Tiptoe through the Tulips"? I remember hearing my mother practice and then play it in a medley of the Golden Oldies of her day (she was born in 1907). In my teens at the time, I thought it was kind of strange. Why would anyone tiptoe through the tulips? When I finally read the lyrics (by Al Dubin in 1929), I discovered it was a love song, in which a guy is asking his gal to "tiptoe through the window" to join him in a moonlight walk to the willow tree, and then through the garden where they tiptoe through the tulips. But why are they tiptoeing? Maybe to avoid stepping on the tulip flowers—or maybe because it's well after dark and his gal isn't supposed to be out with her lover.

I don't remember hearing the song again until Tiny Tim came along. He sang "Tiptoe..." in his falsetto voice first in 1968, and then throughout his career. I never liked anybody's falsetto voice, but especially his, so I never felt nostalgic when hearing it.

That doesn't mean I didn't like tulips, however. I always did and still do love this member of the lily family, which blesses us for a few days each spring—though only in colder-climate habitats (such as the US Northwest). My family was living in Idaho Falls when Mom first played that medley. Perhaps it inspired her to plant a small border bed of tulip bulbs that fall. The bed was along the front of the house, just below my bedroom window, so when those few days came the following spring, I had my own special view of them. I never gave a thought about climbing through the window, though, since my room was on the second floor!

Mom cut the blooms, a few at a time, and put them in vases in the living room and on the dining room table. The colorful blossoms brought spring into the house. My favorite tulip colors were, and still are, red and yellow. I'm not sure if she dug up and replanted the bulbs in the fall or bought new ones, but we had tulips for three more springs—until we moved to Manila, definitely not a clime for tulips.

Most people think that tulips originated in the Netherlands, but that's not so. They came from central Asia and weren't introduced in the Netherlands until 1593. I saw tulip fields there in 1956, but they were bare. I first saw fields of tulips in 2002, while visiting our daughter Jill in Mt. Vernon, WA! Maybe they lured us to Bellingham!

Scribblings

Short seven minute timed pieces, written while together, using an internet random word generator, for the five word prompts.

OFFER, SOLVE, SMALL, SAIL, IMAGINARY

George Francis Edward

If you're a writer, you live part of the time in an **imaginary** world. You create **small** characters to populate that world. Like the real world, your characters have problems to **solve**. You cannot **offer** your own solutions to your characters' problems. They must figure it out. In the end, your characters earn their own independence, and **sail** away from your imaginary world—forever.

Elizabeth Jane Pryce

I always had a great **imagination** for adventurous journeys! I loved to **sail**, and way before I actually was on sailboat I would sit in a tree and imagine the waves and the wind in my hair the salt water burning my eyes and my back glistening with the salt crystals. One day I met a young woman who had been on a boat all her life. She was **small** and had beautiful golden hair . What I noticed the most was the tiny ring of golden wisps on her legs! She **offer**ed to take me out for a spin on the clear blue water. It was my first time on a boat. My dreams were now dis**solve**d into the real thing.

Sandra J. S. Stanton

I was relaxing in my lounge chair on the deck of our **small** cabin by the lake, trying to **solve** the mystery in the book I was reading, before I read the author's solution. Then a friend **offer**ed to take me for a **sail** on the lake. Just then, a loud noise awakened me. Guess I had dozed off. There was no friend in sight. It was just an **imaginary** offer.

Sita Amba-Rao

I had a great desire, a fantasy to go **sail**ing in a **small** sail boat, by myself in the beautiful Bellingham Bay waters, with a book. If I had a choice, right now, that book would be "Becoming" by Michelle Obama. But I was way down the wait list for the book. Luck be it, a friend who had the book and read it, **offer**ed to loan it to me. Perfect, I thought, that would **solve** my problem. Oh! But what about the sail boat? Dang, no boat. Oh, well, never mind, my group forced me to write. So, I said to myself "Go on an **imaginary** sail, in an imaginary boat, on imaginary water with an imaginary book!

GLANCE, BEAM, ENCOURAGE, BORDER, INNOVATE

George Francis Edward

At a quick **glance**, I **encourage**d my wife to plant her flowers on the front deck. "It's a gorgeous day," I say, "you should plant today." My wife plants ten pots of plants, each one containing flowers and fern **border**s. Dana loves to **innovate** with her flower varieties. When she's done, we both step back to appreciate her mastery. Dana **beam**s with pride, as well she should!

Elizabeth Jane Pryce

The **border** patrol guy was big and burly. He sauntered out to the car asking for our green cards and asked whether we had bought anything in Canada. He seems as though he was **beam**ing with a friendly smile until he **glance**d at my son's girlfriend's passport. Suddenly he slammed the windscreen with his hand and shouted at her to get out of the car! We all got out to be able to offer **encourage**ment. It was all a terrible mistake…the dates on her passport was different from the one on her license! He certainly wasn't very **innovative** in his actions.

Sandra J. S. Stanton

Jim and I were looking for a new house, hopefully one with **beam** ceilings. After a week or two, our real estate agent called to say he had found one he was sure we would like. We made an appointment to see it.

Once inside we immediately looked up at the beams. Jim gave me an **encouraging** smile, and I took another **glance**. They were very attractive—a nice dark brown against the creamy white ceiling, but I wondered if we might make their appearance more **innovative** by adding wooden **border**s of the same brown to frame the top of the wall where the beams met it. Yes, that would be the perfect finishing touch. We toured the rest of the house and found it very appealing, but it was those beams that led to our decision to buy.

Sita Amba-Rao

I took a **glance** at one of the gardens on my walk one evening. Wow! The intricate design and arrangement of the plants and shrubs, with the colors, patterns reflecting light, with the sun **beam**ing on their surface! The **border** plants were full of fragrance. The whole arrangement was so **innovative**. It **encourage**d even me, one without a green thumb, to try to work on at least a tiny part of my garden. Off I went home to try.

TRAVEL, PRINT, DISEASE, DOOR, TREAT

George Francis Edward

When you **travel** abroad, you should get all your shots or else, you'll risk contacting a disease. The U.S. Embassy used to have **print**ed travel warnings, but now you can get all this information online. Once you arrive at your destination, and exit the **door** of your apartment or hotel, you will be **treat**ed to the fact you won't be visiting a hospital with some contagious disease.

Elizabeth Jane Pryce

I had to **travel** quite a long way to get to the specialist doctor that had been recommended. I was nervous and worried about this strange **disease** that I had contacted while I was traveling in the Amazon. Would the doctor be able to **treat** me? I wanted to continue roaming for a few more years at least.

After seeing me for a few minutes he handed me a **print**ed sheet with instructions and showed me to the **door**!

Sandra J. S. Stanton

I walked through the glass **door** into the **travel** agency, attracted by the stunning color **print**s of islands in the Caribbean covering the walls. It would be such a **treat** to spend a week or so at any one of them, but perhaps better yet to move from one to another. However, I had read several stories recently about tourists being stricken by **disease** on some islands. I'd better find out which these were so I can avoid them.

Sita Amba-Rao

Air **travel** is always a **treat** for me. I just go on the internet, book the ticket, **print** it out and file it, till the time of travel. Then all I have to do is say, "au revoir" and get out the **door**! It is almost like an addiction for me—feeling high, a delightful **disease**!

BRAIN, GOVERNMENT, LIKE, LINEN, COUGH

George Francis Edward

If you have no **brain**, a career in **government** might be just the ticket for you. Recent polls show only 13% of Americans **like** the U.S. Congress. However, the U.S. dollar is not made of paper, it's comprised of **linen**. You may be asking what does a poll of the unfavorability of Congress and linen dollar bills have to do with each other? Search me—**cough**, cough—I'm only the writer!

Elizabeth Jane Pryce

My grandmother told me a story about the Irish **linen** table cloths used at **government** house parties. The silky white embossed patterns must have been beautiful and I would have **like**d to have seen it. But then, she went and spoilt the whole setting of grandeur I was imagining, by telling me about a gentleman who had a **cough**ing fit and spewed food all over the set table. It was so disgusting it made my **brain** hurt!

Sandra J. S. Santon

Maybe my **brain** is misinterpreting what those **government** guys are saying in their eternal investigations, but I don't **like** anything I hear. Surely even the investigators themselves don't always like what their colleagues say, but they don't speak up and say so—just pull out a **linen** handkerchief and **cough** in disapproval.

Sita Amba-Rao

I **like linen**-ware. But, somehow it seems like they give me a **cough** whenever I am in them, some kind of allergy, I suppose. I racked my **brain** to determine the cause. Searched all the **government** and other media websites and archives, but not a clue as to what was happening. Has anyone any **brain** out there in the government to get me some answers?

STOMACH, MINDLESS, TEARS, NAIL, KNIT

George Francis Edward

I cannot **stomach** horror films. They seem to consist of **mindless** plots, ending in gruesome mutilations, and/or deaths. I never see a horror film with any humor, or pathos. They don't shed **tears**—they prefer violence. I also don't appreciate guns or knives as plot devices. Although a **nail** gun might be interesting. Again, I don't mean to (**k**)**nit**pick, but horror films need a lot of improvement before I'll become a fan!

Elizabeth Jane Pryce

The **mindless** act of **knit**ting , knit one , purl one is often used at elder care centers to help keep elderly peoples hands active and thus free of arthritis. But I have little **stomach** for the such activities. My mother finds it useful at the age of ninety to crochet, she was very **tear**ful when she did not think her son wanted her to make any more blankets for the orphanage. Fortunately he told her he was sorry he had forgotten to collect the blankets already made and asked her to please continue make them. He certainly hit the **nail** on the head, metaphorically, when he told her, because she is now happy that she has something to do again!

Sandra J. S. Stanton

I came home **tear**ful from a trip to the store. A rude shopper, **mindless** of what she was doing, ran straight into me. The **knit**ting needles she had carelessly crammed upside down into her bag, jabbed me right in the **stomach**. One stuck into me so hard it felt like a **nail**. Jim gave me a Kleenex and poured me a glass of wine. I was soon happy again.

Sita Amba-Rao

When I was writing my doctoral dissertation, days and weeks would pass by before I could get the attention of my two advisors. Their **mindless** corrections of the draft, one vetoing the other's English grammar, would make me **tear**ful. It felt like **nail**s piercing my **stomach**. For diversion from this torture I would go to my friend's home and learn **knit**ting, turning it into a sweater for my husband. It ended up into double his size, but we had fun laughing about it before she helped me rectify it!

ABAFT, OPTIMIZE, RESELL, ACHIEVE, SLEET

George Francis Edward

I think it would be great to be an under-**achieve**r. You never have to expect your success, indeed, you could bank on your eventual failure. I wouldn't **optimize** my life by hoping for a miracle if I'm an under-achiever. Instead of going forward; I would look forward to going **abaft**. I might sell my life short as an under-achiever, in fact, I'd **resell** it for a sure failure. Finally, they say everyone hopes for a rosy and a sunny future, but for an under-achiever—rain, snow and **sleet** is all she wrote!

Elizabeth Jane Pryce

Abaft is the daftest sounding word I have heard in a long time! What is wrong with referring to the back of a ship as the stern? Maybe it was only created to **optimize** the use of the alphabet and generate more words! I think it was an over **achieve**r who made that decision. Maybe He or She was bored at the time, maybe the rain had turned to **sleet** and it was probably going to turn to snow soon. They had to think of the selling and **resell**ing of all the dictionaries that would be produced over time! What a lot of nonsense but fun to write something that flows out of such absurdity.

Sandra J. S. Stanton

One way to **optimize** your savings is to look for bargain buys at garage sales and then **resell** your purchases for a profit. We did this for a while and eventually found ourselves with enough savings to go on a cruise. That was quite an **achieve**ment, we thought. However, the cruise was to Alaska in late autumn. One cloudy afternoon, **sleet** was falling, and the deck was slippery. A barrel of who knows what rolled past us, heading **abaft**.

Sita Amba-Rao

I teased my friend who had had a great round the world trip in her youth, saying, "You want to boast about your teenager years, a sneaky drinking adventure **abaft** in the ship, on your round the world voyage? Then go write your story, sell and **re-sell** it to the entire college sororities. To **optimize** your publicity on what an **achieve**r you were, and to show off to your female classmates and friends!"

SLOPE, LUXURIATE, WOEBEGONE, EXCITING, CHASE

George Francis Edward

As a young child, I led an **exciting** life pretending to be a superhero. I dressed in a **woebegone** attire—an old sheet was my cape, my pajamas was my uniform, and I carried a stick for a sword! Nothing **luxuriant** about this superhero…I **chase**d myself around the house. One time our mailman came to our front door, took one look at me, and laughed so hard he almost fell off our front porch. I watched him snickering down the **slope** of our driveway. He was anything but afraid of my superhero costume. It was then it occurred to me I probably looked like another stupid, little kid. My childish superhero bubble was burst!

Elizabeth Jane Pryce

I am heading down a slippery **slope** beginning to write about such a strange mixture of words. I would love to lie back and **luxuriate** in the idea of seeing everyone's **woebegone** face if I didn't write anything at all, but I can't allow myself to do that today. It is more **exciting** to try and try again as my mother would always tell me. But what about the **chase**? Ah, where would we be without that idea!

Sandra J. S. Stanton

Bobby and I were engaged in an **exciting chase** after our dog, Willy, who had escaped under the fence and was heading down the **slope** to the river. Willy's **luxuriant** coat gleamed in the sun. We knew he would come back, but the chase was fun—that is until we saw a small child walking toward us as Willy ran by him. About a five years old, the little boy's **woebegone** expression betrayed sadness or trouble. We knew we had to stop and help him.

Sita Amba-Rao

It was **exciting** to **chase** the deer as it sprinted down the **slope**, although it seemed **woebegone**.

But as we approached the deer at the foothill we found that it had coolly settled on the **luxurious**, grassy field. It looked so content and confident that we just shot a picture and left.

DINING, AWAKE, FORCE, SHINY, ANCIENT

George Francis Edward

Years ago, I bartended late at night and grew accustomed to **dining** later in the evening, sometimes half-**awake**. I would **force** myself to stay awake when driving home. Thank goodness for the **shiny** street lights along my route. That night I would sleep like the dead, and next morning awaken like the **Ancient** Mariner.

Elizabeth Jane Pryce

The **ancient dining** car was all spick and span, clean and **shiny**. One could, if one really wanted to of course, eat off the floor! I didn't want to do that though. I was happy to sit in a beautifully draped chair and sit properly to the table. The work **force** or servers were very attentive, **awake** and alert with big happy smiles, looking pleased to serve all of us dining that day.

Sandra J. S. Stanton

While living in Spain, we decided to go to the parador (an **ancient** castle) in Avila for dinner on my thirty-third birthday. Their décor included a suit of armor, standing in the lobby, tarnished with age but kept **shiny** nonetheless. The ambience was fun, and the menu offered fine **dining**. On this occasion, however, our dinner was late in arriving, though the wine had been delivered right away. One sip led to another, until I had drunk so much wine that I could barely **force** myself to stay **awake**.

Sita Amba-Rao

The **ancient** castle was turned into a **shiny**, new hotel, where people were **awake**ned with a sumptuous breakfast, brought by a lovely attendant, who almost **forc**ing her way in. It was to please the guest who **dine**d on the food with great delight!

SMALL, WEAK, ABRUPT, EXCELLENT, OIL

George Francis Edward

I have an affinity for **small**, **weak** animals—particularly the baby bunny rabbits living in our yard. I watch them each morning. If they **abrupt**ly change their behavior, I look around for the predatory, the neighborhood cat. Her name is Emma and she is a large cat. When I spot Emma, I shout at her to scram or else I toss pebbles. I'm an **excellent** shot. I'm the bunny's protector! I hope someday to be repaid for my kindness—maybe with frankincense, myrrh, or precious **oil**s!

Elizabeth Jane Pryce

There was a **weak** joint in the **oil** pipe, which needed fixing, yet the people in charge kept putting it off. It would have only been a **small** job and would have only taken a short time by a single but **excellent** worker. Instead the break, when it happened, was **abrupt** and violent, sending oil many feet into the air and causing a fire of monumental catastrophe.

Sandra J. S. Stanton

Bob came to an **abrupt** stop when he saw the **small** and obviously **weak** puppy crossing the road. Though he had been on his way to get an **oil** change, Bob decided that rescuing the puppy was an **excellent** opportunity to fulfill his good deed of the day.

Sita Amba-Rao

I recently had knee surgery. The healing was coming along fine, especially at the incision and the resulting stitches. But then, I noticed an **abrupt** change in one spot on the gash—just a **small** and a **weak** one, it appeared. I was concerned that it would open up, but I used my home remedy. I applied an ayurvedic (herbal) **oil** which is an **excellent** treatment for many skin problems. After a few applications, I noticed that the change I saw was merely a scab, which had fallen off and the skin was clearing up. The oil kept the scab moist and eventually helped it come loose. I was relieved. All's well that ended well!

GLISTENING, BRANCH, VIGOROUS, STICK, VAGUE

George Francis Edward

I remember when we opened our brand new, **glistening** Whatcom Educational Credit Union **branch** in Ferndale. I was in charge of conducting our first emergency, evacuation drill. At the sound of my whistle, all employees **vigorous**ly marched out the front door to some **vague** assembly area in the parking lot. There were a few stragglers, but I didn't need to prod them along with a **stick**—I had my trusty whistle!

Elizabeth Jane Pryce

The divining **stick**, my father was using was **glistening** with raindrops as it **vigorous**ly indicated that there was water underground. He threw the **branch** down and ordered the men to start digging. The men did not understand, they were **vague** about the ways of divining.

Sandra J. S. Stanton

I had a **vague** idea that a **branch** halfway up the oak tree would make a fine walking **stick**, but it would require a **vigorous** climb up to get it. By the time I made it up and down on that hot day, my entire body was **glistening** with sweat.

Sita Amba-Rao

I **vague**ly remember that as children, some of my friends and I went into each others' backyards to play. We ran around looking for berries or other fruits. Being summer, the trees were heavy with a variety of fruits. The sun shone brightly and the **branch**es swayed in the wind. The sun **glisten**ed through the leaves, forming interesting patterns on the ground. The tamarind tree was full of ripe pods. We shook the branches **vigorous**ly with **stick**s, until hundreds of them fell to the ground. We gathered and shared among us and took them home to our mothers' who were delight to see the fresh ripe tamarinds ready for use in cooking.

The Newspaper Challenge

Writing generated from a partial sentence taken from a newspaper.

CLOWN SHOES OR SOMETHING?

Sita C. Amba-Rao

*I*t was the year 1954, in India. It was around March. Shaila was eighteen. Her father announced that a special guest would be visiting them for a day, and that they should treat him as a family member. He was addressing Shaila in particular! "Hmm" she pondered, "why me?" She was suspicious. It turned out that the guest was her suitor for marriage. He was a young man, yet much older than Shaila. But that didn't matter. "She was young and dumb anyway" she thought. "Just do what you are told!"

She must have been wearing clown shoes or something, although no such wisdom dawned on her at that time. You know, it is 1954, not 1994, when you really have to be an absurd clown shoe not to use your own thinking, but just follow the rules.

There is more behind this story. Shaila's dad was himself relatively young. He was a good amateur tennis player. In those days almost anyone you would call a professional was into tennis as a hobby. Then there was Amar, the guest, who like Shaila's dad played tennis. They both enjoyed the game. So, Shaila's dad said to Amar, "Come on over for a visit, let's play a game; the winner gets to treat the loser!" He was unconventional in some ways, but he had an ulterior motive. If you use your imagination, you can guess; his motive was to bait Amar as a potential son-in-law!

Not suspecting any of the background to this contrived invitation, Amar accepted it. But then, a caveat! He said, he did not have much time to visit, because he was on a whirlwind tour in search of a bride! For you see, at that time, he was also visiting another city to meet a prospective bride.

Does this bride-matching seem like clown shoes or something? No, don't rush to such a conclusion. Rather, it is quite a rational process, based on the peculiar, unique perhaps, Indian traditional, social norms—tweaked to the individual approaches and realities of the two men.

Here is how the traditional matrimonial system worked: the young woman comes of age, which varied between the ages of fourteen and twenty at that time. She is introduced to other families with young, potential grooms, during public occasions, such as parties or weddings. Alternately, enquiries and information regarding the youngsters and their families are exchanged through social networking. Afterwards, mediators bring the families together. After checking eligibility of the families, including the youngsters and their astrological compatibilities, an agreement is reached—or the process is broken off, and they move on for further search.

In the current case, however, there is a fusion of old and new approaches. Shaila's dad had been exposed to the Western influence, he had spent time in America. He had his own way of finding a match for his daughter. Also, he felt that he had to be selective; he was worried about finding a man of suitable height for his tall daughter! Her height of 5'6" was indeed unusual.

As for Amar, he had no parents, he was in his late 20s and was his own man. His mother had recently passed. He had had a bet with a friend that he would not marry as long as his mother was alive, as he wanted to take care of her. Now that she passed, he was eager to find a wife. He had advertised his requirements in the Matrimonial section of a newspaper:

"Wanted, a tall, hard working girl for a class one officer." Well! My guess is that Shaila was the only tall girl he found!

Thus, the two men's plans worked perfectly, like Clown Shoes—as perhaps some contemporary, self-confident, audacious young men and women would want. Or…? I leave it to your imagination.

The end result was, the young man came, saw and agreed! The wedding was in August of that same year. He took his bride away to the delight of parents and family. Shaila followed with nary a word. What was she thinking? Nothing, I guess. Father knew best, mother too. Her close, older brother was happy. Everyone said Amar was a good man. They deserved each other. So, she went along. Was she wearing clown shoes or something? Maybe, maybe not!

IT'S LIKE WEARING CLOWN SHOES OR SOMETHING

George Francis Edward

$\mathcal{I}$n 2000, my first year working at Western Washington University (WWU), I refused to wear a Halloween costume. As part of an over-the-top response, my boss, who owned several horses, came into my office with a bunch of coworkers, placed a lasso around my neck, and threatened to hang me if I didn't dress up for Halloween. Needless to say, her message was received loud and clear. That was the last time I declined to wear a costume at WWU!

Here I am posing with Elaine, who was a wonderful supervisor. Elaine dressed up as a witch. I told everybody my name was "King George" and I was recently released from the State Mental Hospital. When people talked to me, I requested they bow down and get on their knees. A couple of them complied, which was surprising to me… I have to say I enjoy gushing adulation.

Elaine and I still stay in touch, and regularly have lunch together. I told Elaine I was going to put this photo on Facebook, and she said "I don't care, George! Do it!" Not too many people have as much reckless abandon as Elaine.

After I left Western Washington University, and became Risk Management Officer at the Whatcom Educational Credit Union, I stopped dressing up for Halloween. I figured nobody would place a rope around my neck if I didn't wear a costume! When my fellow workers asked me if I intended to wear a costume for Halloween, I responded "I don't need props for my own self-humiliation." Very true.

Dressing up for Halloween is like wearing clown shoes or something.

Oh, don't get me wrong. I have dressed up on many occasions, but always when I was forced to wear a costume. The photo at left was taken in November 1985. I was bartending in San Diego and I was a huge San Diego Padres fan. So, I dressed up as a mission friar! Makes sense, right?

As 'Father George,' I recall making wisecracks to my bar customers. I would tell them if they didn't tip me, I would make sure they were going straight to Hell! Or after they gave me a fat tip, I would place my hand on their head and say, "Bless you, my son!" It's amazing how wearing a costume makes you say and do things totally out of character. I guess drinking booze has the same effect!

My whole life I have tried NOT to stand out in appearance. Blending in with the crowd was my way of maintaining my anonymity. I was shy as a teenager, and I shied away from any undue attention.

I recall one time my Mom mistakenly purchased a pair of new jeans for me; however, she accidentally bought a pair of jeans with a "side zipper." I tried them on and immediately realized something was wrong, there was no front zipper! "I can't wear these, Mom," I exclaimed. "I think these jeans are made for a girl!"

Mom had been removed from anything stylish for the last few decades. I couldn't rely on her advice for teenage fashion. As an adolescent boy, honestly, I didn't know much about fashion, but I did recognize which were guy's pants, and which pants were for girls.

"Oh, Georgie," Mom explained, "you can hardly see the side zipper."

"That's not the point," I said. "I don't want to take the chance my friends will see me wearing a pair of girls' jeans!" I took the pants off and handed them back to Mom.

My Mom relented and returned the jeans.

I was wearing my new boys' pair of dungarees in High School when the Vice Principal, Mr. Larro, spotted me. "What are you wearing?" he asked. He looked up and down at my denim jeans. "Were you raised in a barn?" Mr. Larro was offended by my appearance. Of course, the Vice Principal always dressed in black like an undertaker, so in his world, I might as well appear sans pants, or buck naked.

Mr. Larro hadn't received the memo saying it was all right for students to wear blue jeans. Mr. Larro still viewed cotton fabrics as signs of a rural upbringing, milking cows and doing farm work. I guess it took a few months for the school administration to approve the dress code changes.

I remember Mr. Larro didn't know who I was. That's because he was in charge of detention and so far, I had avoided attending his detention class. He took me to the Principal's Office, looked up my record and then called home to advise my Mom that he was sending me home to change my pants.

I remember thinking "At least I wasn't sent home for wearing girls' pants!"

For school administrators, it was a losing battle. Pretty soon all the kids were wearing jeans. The floodgates opened, and the great 'Levi sea change' swept over the land.

By the time I graduated high school, dress codes were exploding. Dungarees were in style. Jeans, t-shirts and tennis shoes quickly became de rigueur. However, some hippies chose to run around barefoot.

In 1971 when I graduated from the Wharton School of Finance, I posed wearing a tie and jacket in front of Dietrich Hall. If you look closely, I am barefoot!

Fourteen years later, the music channel, MTV, was born. MTV's entire dress code was contained in just one memorable phrase: "No frontal nudity." When you think of it, with a dress code like that, almost anything goes!

Clown shoes—and all shoes for that matter—were passé. Clown control to Major Tom!

ITS LIKE WEARING CLOWN SHOES OR SOMETHING?

Elizabeth Jane Pryce

$\mathcal{I}$ had the wonderful opportunity to grow up enjoying the tender indulgence of much older and wiser parents, my biological grandparents. But there was another side to the wonderfulness, a conflicting and confusing old-world colonialism. The physical outward showing of affection, or talking to a child about 'life,' were not in character for either of them.

Good behavior was important. For the most part, I should be seen but not heard; that meant I must never be loud, rude, answer back, or have an opinion that conflicted with their deep-seated beliefs of right or wrong. Neither of them were known to raise their voices, but Mummy's sarcasm was never kept in check. At the same time, she would also say, "Sarcasm is the lowest form of wit!"

Mummy was a strong woman, mentally, physically and emotionally. She had been a pioneer in the Australian outback after WWI, living in tents and mud-floor cabins while raising four children. When her youngest was barely two, they crossed the Equator on their way to the Caribbean, a three month journey. Their lives in a few trunks.

There was a constant reminder not to show weakness; "Take a deep breath; pick yourself up; dust yourself off; and start all over again," was a favorite of Mummy's. This did little to comfort my bruised body and ego. But when I was seriously injured, and was taken to a drunk doctor to be stitched up, then Mummy wrapped her arms around me protectively, her face tight with anger against the doctor!

If Daddy came home drunk, she would glare at him and draw her finger across her throat! She'd say, "I'd sooner slit my throat than look at you!" Or, "If looks could kill." It was her way of saying she was angry and disgusted with him. In contrast, if I was upset by another child, she would tell me, "Sticks and stones may break your bones, but words will never harm you." In other words, grow up and take responsibility for yourself.

Mummy loved quotes. She used many of them in my young life. It is very interesting to look them up in the present time, now I am at the age she was, when I was a young girl.

Mummy would take on anyone who she thought was selfish, cruel, or just plain thoughtless. She once slapped me upside the head so that I bounced from one side of the door frame to the other for being cheeky. She was intolerant of Daddy's drinking, yet she'd spend an hour or more guiding a drunk black man through the fields to his home, instead of leaving him to sleep it off. Maybe she couldn't tolerate his pathetic cries for help, "Help me, I be turn'd about and lost, Oh Lard, help me," Or maybe, it was because Daddy, being white, should rise above such behavior.

I never saw, but heard stories about Mummy driving right up behind two women, who refused to move out of the street, oblivious to the horn and hitting them gently with the bumper of the car. That apparently brought screams and wails of, "Oh Lard, she mash me." No one was hurt, and, because she was a white woman in a British colony island, there was no reprimand.

The animals where we lived were not dangerous, but a fat, four foot long snake, devouring my teddy bear, was still a terrifying spectacle. When I ran screaming to Mummy, she was not understanding or sympathetic. She just told me not to be a silly girl!

I realized much later, that she was probably worrying over Daddy, who, at the time, was very ill with DDT poisoning.* The house was kept dark for months, and Daddy stayed in the bedroom until he was better.

Mummy never explained what was happening, or allowed me to see him. By not telling me anything, I believe now, she thought she was protecting me from the pain and grief of adult affairs.

What might have happened if he had never gotten better is beyond my comprehension, even now! It was a very scary time for me, as I felt rejected on all sides, not knowing what was wrong. I became a "problem child" for a while then, engaging in sadistic bursts of anger at my cat, Wong, for no reason, and silent retreats into myself for days.

---

* DDT (dichloro-diphenyl-trichloroethane) was developed in the 1940s as a synthetic insecticide. It was used with great effect to combat malaria, typhus, and the other insect-borne human diseases. It also was effective for insect control in crop and livestock production. In 1962, Rachel Carson's Silent Spring, caused widespread concern over the dangers of improper pesticide use and the need for better pesticide controls.

In contrast, they both did many things for me that made me feel special. Daddy, always polished our shoes until they shone. Mummy made me dresses that were pretty, and even allowed me to wear trousers when I rode a bicycle. The Christmas I was eleven, Daddy built me a beautiful bungalow dollhouse with a verandah. Mummy made the furnishings, complete with armchairs, tables and curtains. She clothed two dolls, one in a dress and one in pants and a jacket, it even had a beard! I sang out of tune carols, and they smiled!

As I grew older, Mummy never discussed my developing body, and the necessary items of clothing I would need. She believed telling a child these things would remove their innocence! However, I remember her talking about her own monthly bleeding. It was horrific. It was Mummy's older daughter, Anne, (my favorite sister), who told me the facts of life, but in such a way, that I believed I would have a child, whether or not I wanted one, by the time I turned twenty-one! It was Anne who also bought my first bra and sanitary pads.

The final conundrum, and the most complex, happened after I left the Caribbean and went to England. It would be fun, I thought, I was only going for a year. I would be returning to my island home and friends. However, within the first three months in England, I was told that, "Mummy" was actually my grandmother, and the person I thought was another sister, was actually my real mother. I was given no choice but to live with her and her four children, and not return to the Caribbean.

With the confusion of "Do what I say, not what I do," during my early life, and the turmoil of all the truths I had ever known being turned upside-down, at age fourteen I no longer felt comfortable in my own skin or being around my contemporaries.

It has only been in recent years that I have gained a better understanding of who I am. The random quote from the newspaper, "Its like wearing clown shoes or something," expresses the emotions I felt growing up: the weirdness of never knowing what was correct: whether to laugh or cry. I did laugh when I was younger, but after I arrived in England, I cried, at least internally, most of the time. I had lost everything familiar and secure in my life.

A COMEDY OF ERRORS

Sandra J. S. Stanton

$\mathcal{W}$ill and I graduated together from UCLA in 1961. But we moved on and never attended a single alumni reunion. Then, in early 2001, we received an invitation to a special reunion honoring graduates of the class of '61. "Hey, that's us, Jean. I think we ought to go to this one," Will said so enthusiastically that I had to agree. The big event was to take place at the Campus Hilford Hotel on the weekend of April 1–3, beginning with a dinner dance on Friday night, followed by a host of other events on Saturday that we could attend with friends—if anybody remembered us! Then brunch and home on Sunday. It sounded like fun.

We lived in Bellingham, Washington, so we would have to take a short flight to Seattle, where we would board a BestAir plane to Los Angeles. It would be a short layover, so we didn't mind. We booked our flight and dug out some dress clothes. Fortunately, mold and moths hadn't gotten to them since we left a career in the Foreign Service. As the weekend approached, we packed our good clothes and shoes for the dinner dance, plus casual wear for the rest of the weekend. We decided to wear something in the spirit of the occasion for the flight south, and Will chose to wear his tennis shoes, as usual.

The day came, and we took a taxi to Bellingham Airport, where we spent a good three hours—our flight delayed by the need for some minor repair. So, of course, we were late getting to Seattle—too late to board the L.A. flight. But we were soon rebooked, and it wasn't long before this plane was heading south. The pilot announced that we would be landing in L.A. about 4:00. That would work timewise. However, the farther south we got, the darker the clouds became. A flight attendant told us to fasten our seatbelts. A rainstorm had hit L.A., which meant rough flying—and a delayed landing. It was close to 5:00 when we arrived at the gate.

We hurried to carousel 1, where we had been told to go, only to discover that our flight's baggage had been taken to carousel 3 because of the delay. We moved fast to get there as the bags began to arrive. Other people found theirs and headed out. Will's bag finally circled around, and he grabbed it, but mine was nowhere in sight. When it was obvious that the carousel wasn't bringing any more bags, we headed for the BestAir counter. They were so sorry…it would surely be on the next flight from Seattle, and they would bring it right to the hotel.

So, with Will's bag in tow, we boarded a shuttle to EZ car rental. Being used to our smallish SUVs, that is what Will had reserved. However, we were late, and our car had been given to someone else. All they could offer us was a huge van. All we could do was take it and head out into the traffic in the rain at rush hour. But Will is a good driver, and we made it to the Hilford intact. Once there, however, we found a full parking lot. The only spaces left were in the farthest corner, and it seemed that all the valets were busy or gone. Once again, all we could do was take what was available.

Once parked, it looked like we could take a shortcut to the entrance by crossing the beautifully planted center dividers. I stepped over the curb into the first one, between the plants, and sank into mud, deep enough to squish over the tops of my shoes and down inside, all the way to my toes. I was in tears as Will helped me back onto the pavement, and we took the longcut to the entrance. It was almost 6:30 before we checked in…and no, my suitcase hadn't been delivered. I started to cry again as we got on the elevator. The dinner dance started at 7:00, and I just couldn't see myself entering the dining room in damp, wrinkled travel clothes and squishy, muddy shoes. Will said we'd figure it out.

Once in our room, he told me to get in the shower, while he dried my clothes with a hair dryer. He decided not to wear his suit, since I had no dress to wear. Then he started to work on my shoes—but to no avail. The mud was even under the innersoles. He offered, "You can wear my good shoes, and I'll wear my tennis shoes."

"But Will," I wailed, "your shoes are men's size 12! I wouldn't be able to hold them on my feet! And forget about dancing!"

Well, we had two choices. We could order room service, or we could go down and join the party with our heads held high and laugh before anyone else could, as we told our unbelievable story. We had never been quitters, and this would be no exception. Will poured some wine that he found in the room refrigerator to help get us in a party mood.

I put on my now dry clothes, attacked my hair with a curling iron, and went wild with my cosmetics. Will stuffed the toes of his tennis shoes with socks, which would help keep my feet in place, but also made the toes stick up kind of funny. I put them on, laced them as tight as I could, and tied the remainder of the long laces around my ankles. At 7:25, we walked out the door. As I clumped down the hall toward the elevator, I looked down at my feet in the size 12 tennies and giggled, "It's like wearing clown shoes or something!"

We became the center of attention the moment we entered the dining room. Everyone turned to look. The announcer said, "There's got to be a good story behind this. Come on up here! So, we joined him on the dais. After he introduced us as Jean and Will Emerson, we began taking turns telling our tale. Soon, our fellow alumni were laughing with us. At the end, I admitted, "I know we'll have fun finding old friends among you and sharing stories over dinner, but it will be hard to sit at the table and watch everyone else dancing."

Then one woman stood up and said "You won't have to do that. What's your shoe size, Jean? By the way, I'm Susan Rose, and I remember being in Dr. Carson's sociology class with you."

"Oh, yes," I replied, and then said, "seven and a half," wondering at her question.

"OK, ladies," Susan said. "All those wearing size seven and a half shoes will come to Jean's table one at a time and sit out a dance barefoot, while you, Jean, dance in their shoes!"

After dinner, the band started playing dance songs they knew we'd like. And sure enough, shoe volunteers started arriving at our table—so many of them that "I could have danced all night!" Then, men came along, to give Will "a chance to rest his feet" while they danced with me.

About 10:00 or so, a bellboy came in to tell me that my suitcase had been delivered. Will gave him a ten and said, "Please, just take it to our room. We're having too much fun to leave now."

When the music stopped, about 11:00, Will and I went up to the dais and borrowed the mike from the band leader. We had something to say. "We promise to attend every reunion from now on, although we're sure none of them will be as much fun as this one, thanks to all of you!"

HOW TO SPARK JOY

Sita C. Amba-Rao

*P*rompted by the local newspaper article's title, "How to spark joy in some major problem areas," I will address joy in a narrowly defined manner—how to spark joy in a specific area, the loss of a loved one. In my case, the loss of my husband, CL.

Let me first go back about 50 years ago. When my father passed away. I was a young daughter, in my early 30s, who had not seen her father in almost a decade, because of her studies away from home and had been looking forward to relating to him as an adult daughter. The loss was almost unbearable, I also had little in the way of a support group around me. It took me almost five years to be able to go on with life with a semblance of normalcy.

When CL passed in 2013, I was in my late seventies, it was equally unbearable, but my response was very different. I had family and friends always in touch; just their constant presence. I also had financial responsibilities to deal with. That is where I began, with love and support quietly surrounding me. I attended grief sessions, read a great deal on grief and loss of a loved one. I "Spoke" with my husband. Then I began thinking. "How can I live, what will be my purpose?" This time I was more aware. I thought I should not let my grief related behavior bring unhappiness and helplessness to those around me. I felt it was time for me to live for others, while taking care of myself. I could help them fulfill their needs, bring some happiness or joy to their life. I was determined to live my life with this purpose.

As time passed, however, another purpose began to preoccupy my mind and heart: to write about my husband, to recall and record memories of him. My progress is slow and comes in increments. I hope I have the ability and fortitude to complete this task.

To live a life with purpose, I started by trying to live mindfully, with awareness. I have created a check list of various kinds.* I ask myself questions, such as, "Is what I am doing of any help to others?" "Am I being considerate with other people's needs." "Am I judging people?" "Am I forgiving, compassionate, committed, thoughtful and grateful," depending upon the situation. Then I act upon it: giving time, money or other involvement to volunteer activities. I wanted something greater than myself; I wanted to contribute to a cause, to make a difference. This gave me a purpose and in turn, fulfillment and joy.

For example, I started a "Make a Difference Fund" at the University, from which I had retired. Part of it was to give scholarships to underserved students, including the LGBTQ categories.

Some people find happiness after their loved one dies, through their religious beliefs. I asked three people at my breakfast table one morning as to how they regained joy after their spouse's died. Two of them said that their belief in God and that their loved one was with the Lord, made them happy. The third said, she had redirected her life into new activities, giving her contentment, if not actual joy.

I reinvented myself by having a family live with me after my husband passed. We mutually took care of each other. While this did not really spark joy, I found a purpose and pursued it. I found contentment and peace with my life.

After losing a loved one, feeling joy is rare, but, I have sparked some happiness through my activities.

* "50 Ways to Add Joy to Your Day," www.psychologytoday.com

THE QUALITY OF MERCY

George Francis Edward

*M*y phone rang, I was informed that a large Isuzu 'cab over truck' had squashed our ATM. Since my job was to investigate all accidents occurring at our Credit Union, I quickly left my Holly Street office and hurried over to our parking lot to inspect the damage. I met our maintenance supervisor and our banking equipment manager in the parking lot.

We have four ATMs in front of our drive up window, each ATM is positioned to allow cars to pull up to perform banking transactions. The striped drive up lanes direct the traffic flow. It is fairly apparent that our ATM drive up lanes are too narrow for a full-size commercial truck. Or so I thought.

A young woman truck driver, just a few months on the job, decided to use her lunch break and visit our ATM. She was driving a large white, Isuzu commercial truck. She couldn't squeeze through the ATM lanes, so she tried to turn around. She misjudged her clearance while backing up. Bad decision, her heavy rig crushed the stand alone ATM, running over it like a pancake.

When I arrived at the scene of the accident, the maintenance supervisor informed me that the woman had to leave because she needed to be back at work. He said she was very sorry for the damage she caused. He was able to write down her name, driver's license and phone number.

The banking equipment manager advised me that the ATM could be repaired. However, he would need to order a new card reader, display and keyboard. He said he'd order those parts as soon as possible. We used a bank equipment supplier in the Midwest.

In the meantime, the maintenance supervisor placed a bright orange traffic cone in our right ATM drive up lane. Now we had three drive up lanes, instead of four.

I reviewed the accident information, which the maintenance supervisor collected. I contacted our insurance company and, as I suspected, we could not submit an insurance claim because our policy contained a $10,000 deductible, and this was a $5,000 claim.

I figured the truck driver was a member of our Credit Union. I checked her account and I found she had less than $100 to her name. No savings account—just a checking account.

I knew our senior management team would expect a full accident investigation report from me, so I did a little background investigation on the young woman driver.

The lady, whom I will call Portia, was a recent graduate of Western Washington University. She was a young mother, married to an unemployed guitar player. It is simply amazing what you can find on the internet!

All of the woman's banking records were in her name. No mention of the child's father. I more or less assumed Portia and her husband were separated; later, when I met Portia, my suspicions were confirmed.

Portia was the proud mother of a two-year old daughter. The little girl was the love of her life, she was the reason Portia worked so hard to support her family.

It was fairly clear to me at this early stage, Portia would not be able to reimburse our Credit Union for the $5,000 damages. Her deposited paychecks barely covered her rent checks.

I wondered if Portia was working two jobs, or perhaps depending on cash loans from her parents (or even her estranged husband).

It turns out Portia never married the guitar player, and there were no alimony payments.

Next, I called Portia and we set up an appointment. About a week passed, and Portia stopped by the Credit Union to meet with me. We met in my office.

Portia was twenty-four years old, with long brown hair and brown eyes. She was slim and sunburned. She worked for a landscape company; besides driving the Isuzu truck, her job description entailed carrying and spreading bags of wood chips and mulch. Occasionally, she used garden tools like hoes and shovels to dig flower beds or irrigation trenches. It was a run-of-the-mill "lunch pail" job—hard, backbreaking work for minimum wage.

However, Portia loved it. She said that after graduating college, she searched for a job for over a year before she found this landscaping position. She got the job because she knew a fellow employee.

Portia graduated from Western Washington University with a degree in psychology. After four years of study, taking useless courses, and two wasted years learning "sentient psychology," landscaping was the only career path available. With a young daughter to take care of, Portia wasn't very picky about where she worked. She just needed a monthly income.

As I interviewed Portia, I could see that she was extremely frightened. Her voice was so quiet I could barely hear her. Undoubtedly, she knew there was no way she could pay for the damages to our ATM.

I asked Portia if her employer was informed about the ATM accident. "No," she said. "If I told them, I'd be terminated." Portia looked down at her feet the whole time she spoke to me.

I explained our process to Portia. We were waiting for the ATM parts to be shipped from the Midwest, and once they arrived in Bellingham, a local security company would do the install. There would be labor charges and the cost of the ATM parts about $5,000 in all.

Portia's face blanched. I could see she was thinking about her job, and maybe her little girl.

Portia left my office and I composed my investigation report to our Senior Management team.

I recommended we absorb all the costs of the ATM repair, and not inform Portia's employer. Portia needed her job more than our Credit Union needed the $5,000. In my report I quoted the soliloquy in the Merchant of Venice. It is spoken by Portia, a Shakespearean heroine:

"The quality of mercy is not strained.

It droppeth as the gentle rain from heaven

Upon the place beneath. It is twice blest:

It blesseth him that gives and him that takes."

Senior Management unanimously agreed with my recommendation. I advised our banking equipment manager to send me the ATM invoices. I would take care of it.

Before I closed my file, I wrote a letter to Portia explaining the decision by our management not to seek restitution from her landscape employer. I thanked her for meeting with me and for giving me honest answers to my questions. I wished her good luck in her future endeavors.

"Blessed are the merciful, for they will be shown mercy." (Matthew 5:7)

CAMERON'S ORPHANAGE PROJECT

Elizabeth Jane Pryce

*Z*ambia is a land-locked African country, with a population of 17 million whose median age is eighteen years.This includes 1 million orphans, according to the United Nations Development Program. At least one in thirteen children is likely to die before reaching the age of five.

In 2001, a couple of trustees from a school in Wales took a group of students on an expedition to Zambia. During this visit, the group came into contact with Mr. Albert Mwansa and two of his colleagues, who were trying to teach around 26 children in a roofless building, in a small region called Itala, meaning 'just across the river.' It was a short distance from the remote village of Mkushi, in the north of Zambia. The group met with the local Chief, and were able to secure a piece of land on which to build the first school building. The land was registered under the new title of the 'Itala Foundation' and became the site of all future projects.

It was here that the first mud and thatch classrooms were built, with room for sixty children. In 2007, the Itala Foundation became a registered charity run by a team of six trustees based in the UK.

I had studied geography as a child growing up in the West Indies with my grandparents and knew about Rhodesia before it was split, becoming Zambia and Zimbabwe. I also had family members who had lived in Rhodesia when it was British, but my first real knowledge of Zambia came from Alexandra Fuller's books about her childhood growing up in Africa. She lived through some of the changes from British dominance to independence.

In 2016 Amanda Jayne, my younger brother's fiancé, took an expedition of young adults to Zambia to work at the Itala Foundation School. They were there repairing and repainting the school walls. While there, Amanda met Marlon Chibuye, who was running the school. He told her in conversation that he if he had enough money, he would build a nursery school and an orphanage.

Only two months previously, Amanda Jayne's son, Cameron Forster, had died in a tragic accident. He was only twenty-one. Amanda saw a perfect opportunity to create a legacy in her son's name and bring joy into a major problem area. Cameron's Orphanage Project was born.

Amanda Jayne and Roniss who will live in the Orphanage and work in the pre-school.

The first group working on the Itala School, stayed in traditional mud huts without electricity or running water. To provide hot water for bathing with at the end of the day, they filled plastic bags with water and left them in the sun.

Everyone who had known Cameron, threw all their energy into raising money to make sure his legacy was completed. By the following year, enough money had been raised to provide a borehole for a second water pump in the village.

During a two week visit in September 2017, twenty-one young adults, who had paid their own way from London to Mkushi, built the orphanage and nursery school up to roof height with bricks they made, fired and laid.

By May 2018, Cameron's Orphanage Project had become its own charity, run by both Amanda Jayne and James White, my brother. In 2019, the inside of the orphanage was finished, curtains made and hung, floors sealed with a locally made formula, and the bunk-beds built and installed.

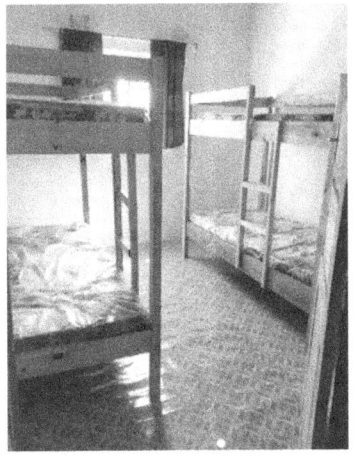

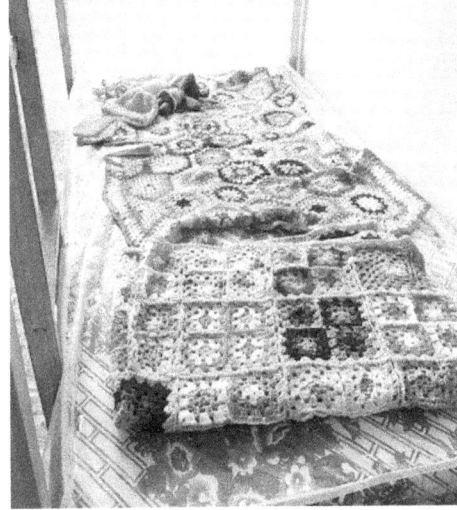

The first children to move in were three year old Ruth and seven year old Awah.

On Awah's bed are the blankets crocheted by my ninety-year-old mother, who is happy to have something purposeful to do with her hands!

I had a new sewing machine and was eager to make some dresses. In the end it was decided that I should make ten uniforms for the school children. I was delighted to receive a picture of a little girl wearing one of the dresses. I will be making more dresses during the winter, but this time, in bright colors and different styles!

TOUGH UNIVERSAL PROBLEMS AND CARING INDIVIDUAL SOLUTIONS

Sandra J. S. Stanton

*I*n every newspaper we read, at least one article alerts us to the suffering of others—whether in our city or country or elsewhere in the world. There are poor people who shiver in old, long-worn-thin clothes. There are hungry people on the streets and families who can't afford to give their children a healthy diet. There are schools with so few books that students must share them. There are elderly who need a helping hand. And let us not forget lost or abandoned animals, who roam the streets or are taken to a shelter that may not have the means to help them.

These are major problems, for which there are inadequate solutions. Whose job is it to provide solutions? Many people say it's up to public or private organizations, but we all know that a lot of these problems simply aren't resolved by bureaucratic entities. Or if they are, the human touch is often lacking. That's what I want to talk about: how we, as caring human beings, can make a difference in this world—bringing joy to others and, in so doing, to ourselves.

How many times have you bought a sweater or jacket, taken it home, and found that it doesn't really suit you. Well, of course you could take it back, but I have another idea, suggested by a friend. Find a way to give it to someone who needs it. If you don't know such a person, take it to a school or church office, for instance, and ask them to find a needy recipient. But before you do, write a note signed "from someone who cares" and attach it to the sweater (or other new item of clothing). The recipient will be all the happier knowing that someone cares about them, and you'll feel good too.

Another friend told me that she often prepares a generously packed sack lunch and puts it in her car when she goes out. Inevitably, she sees someone hanging around a street corner. While they may want money, she gives them lunch instead. If you like, you can put a note in the sack. Another idea: If you know, or know of, a family that has a hard time buying groceries, you could fill a grocery bag, stick in that note, and leave it on their porch.

Our grandson's school class heard that many schools in Liberia lacked books for their libraries. The kids collected enough books to fill a whole pile of boxes! His dad, who once lived in Liberia, helped pack the boxes and arranged for them to be shipped to schools in that country.

Bellingham at Home, a volunteer organization of seniors helping seniors in this Washington town, provides transportation to members who need it. Driving their own cars, the volunteers pull right up to the house, help the person get in the car, take them where they need to go, and then take them home, sometimes offering a stop at the grocery store or library! I am one of those with this need, and I have become good friends with some of "my drivers." A great bonus!

Our daughter Jill and her husband Shawn recently adopted a dog from a shelter in the Bellingham area. They learned that the dog had been picked up on a highway in Oklahoma and taken to the nearest shelter, which already had more dogs than they could manage. However, they contacted an interstate volunteer organization that transports animals to shelters with extra room. Volunteers took this dog and four others to the shelter where Jill and Shawn found their new dog, Masi. How many kind people helped Masi find his new home? Our son Mike and his family foster entire families of kittens in their North Carolina home until the local shelter can find permanent homes for them.

While these problems are universal, the best solutions may be found in individual acts of human caring—making both givers and receivers a little happier.

GIFTS THAT STAND OUT

Sita C. Amba-Rao

*G*ifts! What does that mean? Google's dictionary defines it as a thing freely given without compensation. It means an offering, a contribution or just giving. It can be an expression or an action, showing care and thoughtfulness. These are things that bring us closer to our friends. They could be shared experiences based on our interests, such as culture and travel. Even in a long distance friendship, one can send a gift of love from far away.*

I have around my home, as others do, many tangible gifts from various people. However, given the above criteria of "gifts that stand out," what is significant are my memories of what others have done for me, instead of material objects given to me. I can go back through my memory trove and recall such treasures of love and care.

There is Raj, whose friendship spans more than sixty years. We were both about twenty years old, when we first met in law school. I was one year behind her, so when she graduated and left, I was the only remaining single female student in the college. The year before, there were four of us. While I was alone, preparing for my finals, Raj surprised me one day, by coming to town to see me, and to encourage me in preparing for my exams. She spent a couple of days with me and left me inspired. On one other occasion, a few decades later, she sent a gift of her friendship across the ocean to me in America. This was a "friend-for-ever letter"—A special surprise and gift, as we mostly communicated by telephone.

Raj is just one of several such friends, both individuals and groups, that are bright stars in my life. My City Gym group, for example, the City Peeps, is special. The members lookout for each other while having fun. Yesterday, some of us met for a potluck lunch at one of their homes. Our host Linda, told her husband gleefully, "We dance hard and we eat well!"

* G.C. Ragalo, blog on the Importance of Gift Giving in a relationship.

There is also Nonya and her family, who warmly opened up their home to me for over seven months after CL passed. A place to spend my nights surrounded by companionship. Even now, they still remind me that the room upstairs where I slept was mine to use any time. They continue to invite me into their home with love.

I'll always fondly remember Ruby and her family. They were my surrogate family here in Bellingham for six years after CL passed. Ours was truly a mother and daughter relationship. Often Ruby would sense my need and take care of it before I could even ask.

Finally, there are two young women, Roshni and Angela. Roshni's late mother, Soonu was a dear friend of mine. When I moved from my home recently, the two took the initiative to transport my goods to my new home and arranged the things at the new place, making my transition effortless. They constantly remind me to call as needed; another relationship where the gift certainly stands out in a crowd.

There are so many other friends and family members, right here in beautiful Bellingham and elsewhere, who are my anchors, my rocks for support and inspiration. Yes, rocks can be inspiring too, don't you agree?

Ultimately, individually and collectively, the help of these wonderful people is the gift that has enabled me to continue living in Bellingham.

GIFTS THAT STAND OUT FROM THE CROWD

George Francis Edward

*G*IFT—A natural ability or talent. "He has a gift for comedy."

Sculptor Ron Mueck, was born in Australia. He sculpted Big Man in 2000, from a live model. It was made from polyester resin over fiberglass and cast from a clay base fashioned over chicken wire, then Mueck adjusted the brow to make him look angry.

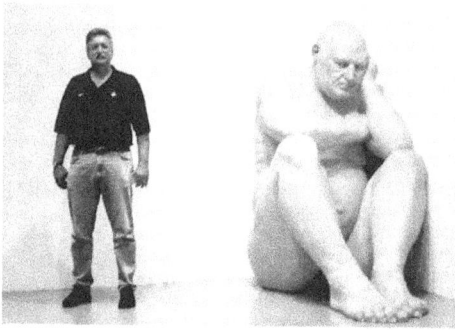

George and "Big Man" by Ron Mueck

To me, Big Man represents the angry man inside of me. Of course, I never want this ugly side of me to appear, but occasionally, it just does. My angry man can be petulant, childish, unreasonable, and sometimes totally bonkers. But it lives and breathes, just like me. When I drank, Big Man would appear quite often.

It is a gift. Of sorts.

Of course, one must control your anger. I remember once when I was driving Heidi Hotpants (my 1970 red Volkswagen), I was pulling out into a lane of traffic in Silver Spring, Maryland. An old man and his wife were driving by in a big Cadillac. For some reason, this driver sped up to cut me off and prevent me from merging into traffic. It was deliberate. He was traveling about 30 mph, and when he saw me signal and attempt to merge into his lane, he hit the gas pedal and zoomed to 50 mph, almost hitting me and preventing my merger.

I went ballistic. I chased this poor man, tailgating him, for about a mile. I flashed my headlights at him and beeped my horn.

My Big Man was in control.

Eventually, I turned off and allowed the poor fellow to continue on his merry way. He probably never realized why I was so mad at him. I'm lucky they didn't have cell phones then, back in 1974, because the beleaguered man could have called the cops on me. Rightfully so.

Don't get me wrong. Two can play this game.

I was attending a wedding in Whittier, California. My good friend from high school, Joe, was marrying his sweetheart, Lena. After the wedding, I was driving back to San Diego.

It was around midnight, and I was lost trying to find the Los Angeles Freeway. Unbeknownst to me, I had on my high-beam, bright headlights. I pulled behind a low-rider vehicle, full of gangbangers. They instantly took offense to my bright headlights.

The gangbangers pulled aside and let me drive by. They then followed me, just a few feet from my back bumper, tailgating me, for what seemed like half an hour. They flashed their headlights and blasted the horn. I was continuously harassed for miles. Eventually, they pulled alongside me, rolled down the windows, and all the gangbangers gave me the finger. They shouted a few things at me in Spanish, and then drove away.

Now I knew how the old man in the Cadillac felt ten years before.

I had to go to traffic school, because I was caught speeding. At the traffic school, the instructor asked us all to recount the infraction that had brought us to the school. For me, it was purely speeding, going 60 in a 35 mph zone.

However, I confessed to the traffic class that this was not my worst offense. I told the class about the incident when I tailgated this poor little man in the Cadillac. I admitted that I didn't receive a ticket then, but I certainly deserved one. I only realized how scary this incident was after I was subjected to the same treatment by the gangbangers.

Yes, you must control the Big Man.

However, sometimes the Big Man can save you from a dangerous situation.

I was in New Orleans, walking down Bourbon Street with my wife, Dana. Some Motorcycle Momma was passed out drunk on the sidewalk. I stepped over her leather-suited body and continued walking. The fellow behind me didn't see the unconscious Momma, and he accidentally kicked her. I think he stepped on her ankle. Motorcycle Momma woke up, and I was the first person she glimpsed. Naturally, she assumed I was the one who kicked her.

She yelled at me, cursing and stumbling. She followed me along Bourbon Street, trying to step on the back of my ankle, to show me how it felt. I told her I hadn't stepped on her leg, or kicked her; it had been somebody else. Momma didn't care, she was going to teach me a lesson. After about a block of this harassment, I had enough of Motorcycle Momma. I turned around, assumed a fighter's pose, and as God is my witness, I would have knocked her unconscious. I screamed at her as I drew back my fist, "Stay away from me, you m-f-$@%! bitch, or I'll f**k you up!!!"

Just at that moment, Motorcycle Momma's boyfriend, who was also drunk, caught up to us and pulled her away. At the same time, my wife grabbed my arm and tried to pull me away from Momma. Momma and I were dragged apart. Everybody was shouting. It was quite the scene, but we went our separate ways, without fists being thrown, or anyone going to jail.

My Big Man might have protected me, maybe. On the other hand, he could have landed me in a whole bunch of trouble. We'll never know.

This is why I keep the Big Man locked up in the basement of my soul. He only comes out when it is absolutely necessary. If I were a better man, more mature, the Big Man would never need to make an appearance. Ever.

I'm working on it.

GIFTS THAT STAND OUT FROM THE CROWD

Elizabeth Jane Pryce

*T*hey laughed and joked a little with their friends when Zoe told them about the letter from the young man who was coming from America. With his funny writing and the way he wrote his words, you could almost hear him tripping over himself in his excitement about coming to London. But it was his last sentence that had really caught Zoe's attention. The time grows short to when my life will change and I will meet you. She didn't understand why, but she felt her stomach tighten and do a small somersault.

When her husband made a comment about Americans being naive and immature, she laughed nervously and cleared the dinner plates from the table. They had enjoyed a wonderful meal of trout in a latticed pastry, with vegetables and roasted potatoes. Zoe stood by the kitchen window and looked down the long garden for a few minutes; she saw and heard the barn owl that had been frequenting their back yard for a few nights now. She was thrilled. All would work out well, she thought, shaking her head slightly—no need for worrying now. They needed the money to work on the house and the American Heritage Society paid host families well.

Zoe prepared the coffee, picked up the cherry cheesecake and returned to the living room. That's where the dining table was set up.

"We were beginning to think you had got lost darling," her husband said, as she walked in the door.

"No such luck," Zoe replied. "I put the coffee on and set the tray. Can you go and get it please while I serve up the dessert. Oh, and bring the mahjong set as well."

"Don't you think Matthew sounds like a nice young man?" Zoe asked, as they both stood in the bathroom cleaning their teeth. They had played a good game of mahjong, and it was now quite late. "He might even be willing to help with the work on the house, don't you think?"

"Oh, yes, He loves old houses! That's what he said wasn't it?" Bill laughed.

Zoe didn't answer, but went to check on the children before getting into bed.

"We'll just have to wait and see what he is like when he gets here on Saturday or Sunday. Gosh, I do hope there isn't a rail strike on the day he arrives." Bill was already snoring lightly.

The following Saturday afternoon, the children were running around chasing each other and shrieking when Zoe thought she heard a knock at the door.

"Hi, I'm Matt," the stranger announced grabbing her hand, as soon as she opened the door. "I am so happy to be here." Zoe was speechless for a few moments, by which time the children had gathered. Little William came up behind her and tucked his hand into hers, while the older two children peered round the wall at the bottom of the stairs, giggling.

"I'm sorry, please come in. Is that all the luggage you have? I'm afraid Bill isn't here at the moment; he had to go into town to buy a few things. Would you like a cup a tea?"

"I'd luv a cuppa tea," he said in a funny English accent, which made James and Jayne giggle and hide their faces in their hands. William just stared with those big blues eyes of his.

"OK kids, don't be silly any more, say hello to Matthew properly."

"Please call me Matt! Now, let me see if I know your names," he said, his eyes sparkling with humor.

William and James went off to play together after a few minutes, but Jayne stayed downstairs, alternately hiding behind the study door and coming out into the kitchen, bursting into a fit of giggles, and running back behind the door.

Bill came home just after they had finished their cuppa, real English style with milk, Matt had also had sugar. In a couple more days, another young man, this time from New York, would be arriving. They would both occupy the large room upstairs. Zoe loved it, because she thought it looked like an old-fashioned dorm room.

The room was painted a pale blue with blue and white checkered curtains at the window, which overlooked the garden out back. She had shopped around while the children were in school for two single beds, which had been delivered last week. They were made up with white cotton sheets, cream wool blankets, which her mother had given her, and machine-appliquéd pillowcases she had made herself. Zoe was most proud of the white candlewick bedspreads she had bought from Jones Brothers on the Holloway Road.

Bill took Matt upstairs, showed him where the bathroom was on the first floor, then up another floor to their room, where he left Matt to organized his few things.

"He's very excitable, isn't he?" Bill said, when he came downstairs. "Typical American!"

"Oh, will you give over; I think it is quite nice to have a bit of over exuberance in the house for a change. It's only for six months anyway, and both of them will be gone most of the day."

"I know, I know. I'm just not too fond of having some other man living in my house and sharing my bathroom." Zoe laughed, "Oh don't be silly; we talked about this. Just remember the money; it will help us considerably. The children seem to like him too, although Jayne is being a silly little goose, giggling and hiding! It might be kind of fun to show someone around London. It would give me something to do with the children, instead of working on the house all the time. I must start dinner. I thought a Quiche Lorraine might be a good idea. What are you going to do?"

"I'll find something," Bill said, and disappeared.

Zoe had just started peeling the potatoes, ready to roast, when Matt, came downstairs. His first words shocked her. "What can I do to help? I am an expert potato peeler if you'd like me to do those?"

"OK," was all Zoe managed to say. Bill had never offered to help her cook dinner, even when she wasn't well! As they worked side by side in the kitchen, never really getting in each other's way, they laughed and chatted about the house, the children, his family, her family. Everything was ready and in the oven in no time.

"Maybe you could show me around your neighborhood, we have an hour don't we?"

"Why not," Zoe replied, "I'll get the children."

"Kids, get your shoes on. We are going to take a walk, show Matt where things are around here." There were cries of excitement as the three children tumbled down the stairs in their haste to go do something fun.

163

Zoe found Bill downstairs in the basement. "We're going to go for a walk. Dinner is cooking in the oven and will be ready when we get back. We're just going for a short walk to the canal and back."

Although she didn't know it at the time, Zoe was about to embark on a journey where the 'gifts' she would receive would last a lifetime and stand out from anything else she would ever experience.

GIFTS THAT STAND OUT FROM THE CROWD

Sandra J. S. Stanton

When I saw this phrase from a newspaper feature title, I began to think of different ways that can make a gift stand out from the crowd. I'm sure there are many more than these that I'm sharing here.

Unlike most of us, Anne loves to shop, especially for gifts—not only on special occasions, but even to thank someone for inviting her to lunch or helping her with a difficult project. And when Anne goes into shopping mode, she doesn't just look around until she finds something interesting. She insists on buying something unique, especially for favorite friends or family members who appreciate her talent for choosing the perfect book, sweater, kitchen gadget, or even garden accessory. When her gifts are opened, two people are made happy, both the recipient and Anne, who strives to make sure her gifts stand out from the crowd.

Sarah would much rather stay home than go shopping, but she still comes up with wonderful gifts. Sometimes she browses the Internet, sitting at her desk, but it's hard to be sure what you're getting if you must choose based on a picture. That's fine in some cases, but Sarah would rather give something she has made. She cooks and bakes, grows herbs and flowers, sews and knits, and sketches scenes from nature. She gives her neighbors a crock of soup with some homemade bread. Her friends often receive flowers, dried herbs, or cookies. Family members are always happy to receive sweaters or other things that Sarah has made in styles and colors she knows they like. Everyone is happy when she gives them a simply framed sketch or pastel of flowers, backyard birds and animals, or sometimes the recipients' pets that she sketches from a photograph. Sarah gives presents that nobody else has, making them stand out from the crowd.

Karen buys her gifts for others. She's good at choosing things they will like, but what makes them special is her talent for wrapping them. Some of her gifts are beautifully wrapped in heavy paper of brilliant colors and designs, then tied with velvet and satin ribbons, or even "ribbon" she has crocheted. Not even the finest stores' gift wrappers can hold a candle to Karen's masterpieces. Other gifts she has fun wrapping, hoping to totally surprise the recipient. She will place a small-sized gift in large box, stuffed with crumpled newspapers, then wrapped in brown paper and tied with string. Or she will create an odd-sized box by taping pieces of cardboard together; these are tough to wrap, but she'll find a way! Once she put two tissue-wrapped towel sets in an ordinary box, which she wrapped with a beach towel and tied with rope! If you receive one of Karen's wrapped gifts, you'll know who it's from, but you won't have a clue what it might be. And whether the wrappings are beautiful or downright crazy, Karen's gifts certainly stand out from the crowd.

So, the next time you want to give someone a gift, put on your thinking cap and find a way to make it "stand out from the crowd."

Author Bios

Sita C. Amba-Rao is a Professor Emerita of Management, School of Business, Indiana University at Kokomo. She has a doctorate degree in Management and Industrial Relations from Purdue University. She taught in Business Schools in Alabama and Indiana. She also worked as Head of Personnel and Human Resources in India. On her retirement in the year 2000, her husband C.L. Amba-Rao and Sita moved to Bellingham. Sita joined the writer's group in 2018, which is helping her work on her literary skills, so she can write about her husband who passed in 2013. She is delighted to live at Solstice Senior Living in Fairhaven.

George Francis Edward graduated from the Wharton Business School and holds a Juris Doctor from USD School of Law. He and his wife, Dana, moved to Washington State in 1999. He served as a Risk Management Officer for a local credit union until 2015. He was the chief fraud investigator, and based on his investigations, he developed a fraud detection

program called WECUSAFE. After his retirement from the credit union, George published a book titled *How to Steal from Mom* in May 2015. In September 2019, the Whatcom County Council appointed George to a three-year term on the Northwest Senior Services Board.

Elizabeth Jane Pryce is a retired landscape artist and award winning gardener. She grew up in the Caribbean with her maternal grandparents, returning to England to live with her mother and siblings when she was fourteen. She moved from London to Bellingham, Washington, with her children in 1991. Her first collection of poems, *Wild Child*, published in 2010, captures the influences that family and nature had upon her. She is also published in two volumes of *Clover*, a literary rag and *Borders: An Anthology of Stories*. She now devotes herself to her garden, writing her memoir and volunteering with Bellingham at Home.

Sandra J. S. Stanton, born in Los Angeles, lived in seven states and five foreign countries before settling in Bellingham with her husband, Jim, and their cat, Silver Dollar, in 2016. Her life abroad has given her much to write about. After graduating from UCLA, she was a writer and editor for the US government and, then, for Sociological Abstracts, LLC.

Since 2012, she has been a freelance writer and editor for Chanticleer Reviews and Media, LLC (in Bellingham) and other clients. In 2018, as a member of Bellingham at Home, she joined The Blue Bottles Writing Studio.